Can't Help It?

Fran and Jill Sciacca

Jim Hancock

David C. Cook Church Ministries—Resources
A division of Cook Communications Ministries
Colorado Springs, CO/Paris, Ontario

Custom Curriculum
Can't Help It?

© 1994 David C. Cook Publishing Co.

David C. Cook Church Ministries—Resources
A division of Cook Communications Ministries
4050 Lee Vance View; Colorado Springs, CO 80918-7100
Cable address: DCCOOK
Series creator: John Duckworth
Series editor: Randy Southern
Editor: Randy Southern
Option writers: Stan Campbell, Sue Reck, and Randy Southern
Designer: Bill Paetzold
Cover illustrator: Marcel Durocher
Inside illustrator: Joe Weissmann
Printed in U.S.A.

ISBN: 0-7814-5148-5

CONTENTS

Sessions by Jim Hancock
Options by Stan Campbell, Sue Reck, and Randy Southern

About the Authors

Jim Hancock is a volunteer youth worker and a writer for IMS Productions in Colorado Springs, Colorado. He has worked on several projects for the youth market, including the *Edge TV* video series.

Stan Campbell has been a youth worker for almost twenty years and has written several books on youth ministry including the BibleLog series (SonPower) and the Quick Studies series (David C. Cook). Among the books he's written in the Custom Curriculum series are *Hormone Helper, Just Look at You! What Would Jesus Do?* and *Your Bible's Alive!* Stan and his wife, Pam, are youth directors at Lisle Bible Church in Lisle, Illinois.

Sue Reck is an editor for Chariot Family Products. She is also a freelance curriculum writer. She has worked with young people in Sunday school classes, youth groups, and camp settings.

Randy Southern is a product developer of youth material at David C. Cook and the series editor of Custom Curriculum. He has also worked on such products as Quick Studies, Incredible Meeting Makers, Snap Sessions, First Aid for Youth Groups, Junior Highs Only, and Pathfinder Electives.

You've Made the Right Choice!

Thanks for choosing **Custom Curriculum!** We think your choice says at least three things about you:

(1) You know your group pretty well, and want your program to fit that group like a glove;

(2) You like having options instead of being boxed in by some far-off curriculum editor;

(3) You have a small mole on your left forearm, exactly two inches below the elbow.

OK, so we were wrong about the mole. But if you like having choices that help you tailor meetings to fit your kids, **Custom Curriculum** *is* the best place to be.

Going through Customs

In this (and every) **Custom Curriculum** volume, you'll find

• five great sessions you can use anytime, in any order.

• reproducible student handouts, at least one per session.

• a truckload of options for adapting the sessions to your group (more about that in a minute).

• a helpful get-you-ready article by a youth expert.

• clip art for making posters, fliers, and other kinds of publicity to get kids to your meetings.

Each **Custom Curriculum** session has three to six steps. No matter how many steps a session has, it's designed to achieve these goals:

• *Getting together.* Using an icebreaker activity, you'll help kids to be glad they came to the meeting.

• *Getting thirsty.* Why should kids care about your topic? Why should they care what the Bible has to say about it? You'll want to take a few minutes to earn their interest before you start pouring the "living water."

• *Getting the Word.* By exploring and discussing carefully selected passages, you'll find out what God has to say.

• *Getting the point.* Here's where you'll help kids make the leap from principles to nitty-gritty situations they are likely to face.

• *Getting personal.* What should each group member do as a result of this session? You'll help each person find a specific "next step" response that works for him or her.

Each session is written to last 45 to 60 minutes. But what if you have less time—or more? No problem! **Custom Curriculum** is all about . . . options!

What Are My Options?

Every **Custom Curriculum** session gives you fourteen kinds of options:

• *Extra Action*—for groups that learn better when they're physically moving (instead of just reading, writing, and discussing).

• *Combined Junior High/High School*—to use when you're mixing age levels, and an activity or case study would be too "young" or "old" for part of the group.

• *Small Group*—for adapting activities that would be tough with groups of fewer than eight kids.

• *Large Group*—to alter steps for groups of more than twenty kids.

• *Urban*—for fitting sessions to urban facilities and multiethnic (especially African-American) concerns.

• *Heard It All Before*—for fresh approaches that get past the defenses of kids who are jaded by years in church.

• *Little Bible Background*—to use when most of your kids are strangers to the Bible, or haven't made a Christian commitment.

• *Mostly Guys*—to focus on guys' interests and to substitute activities they might be more enthused about.

• *Mostly Girls*—to address girls' concerns and to substitute activities they might prefer.

• *Extra Fun*—for longer, more "rowdy" youth meetings where the emphasis is on fun.

• *Short Meeting Time*—tips for condensing the session to 30 minutes or so.

• *Fellowship & Worship*—for building deeper relationships or enabling kids to praise God together.

• *Media*—to spice up meetings with video, music, or other popular media.

• *Sixth Grade*—appearing only in junior high/middle school volumes, this option helps you change steps that sixth graders might find hard to understand or relate to.

• *Extra Challenge*—appearing only in high school volumes, this option lets you crank up the voltage for kids who are ready for more Scripture or more demanding personal application.

Each kind of option is offered at least twice in each session. So in this book, you get *almost 150* ways to tweak the meetings to fit your group!

Customizing a Session

All right, you may be thinking. *With all of these options flying around, how do I put a session together? I don't have a lot of time, you know.*

We know! That's why we've made **Custom Curriculum** as easy to follow as possible. Let's take a look at how you might prepare an actual meeting. You can do that in four easy steps:

(1) *Read the basic session plan.* Start by choosing one or more of the goals listed at the beginning of the session. You have three to pick from: a goal that emphasizes *knowledge,* one that stresses *understanding,* and one that emphasizes *action.* Choose one or more, depending on what *you* want to accomplish. Then read the basic plan to see what will work for you and what might not.

(2) *Choose your options.* You don't *have* to use any options at all; the

basic session plan would work well for many groups, and you may want to stick with it if you have absolutely no time to consider options. But if you want a more perfect fit, check out your choices.

As you read the basic session plan, you'll see small symbols in the margin. Each symbol stands for a different kind of option. When you see a symbol, it means that kind of option is offered for that step. Turn to the options section (which can be found immediately following the Repro Resources for each session), look for the category indicated by the symbol, and you'll see that option explained.

Let's say you have a small group, mostly guys who get bored if they don't keep moving. You'll want to keep an eye out for three kinds of options: Small Group, Mostly Guys, and Extra Action. As you read the basic session, you might spot symbols that tell you there are Small Group options for Step 1 and Step 3—maybe a different way to play a game so that you don't need big teams, and a way to cover several Bible passages when just a few kids are looking them up. Then you see symbols telling you that there are Mostly Guys options for Step 2 and Step 4—perhaps a substitute activity that doesn't require too much self-disclosure, and a case study guys will relate to. Finally you see symbols indicating Extra Action options for Step 2 and Step 3—maybe an active way to get kids' opinions instead of handing out a survey, and a way to act out some verses instead of just looking them up.

After reading the options, you might decide to use four of them. You base your choices on your personal tastes and the traits of your group that you think are most important right now. **Custom Curriculum** offers you more options than you'll need, so you can pick your current favorites and plug others into future meetings if you like.

(3) *Use the checklist.* Once you've picked your options, keep track of them with the simple checklist that appears at the end of each option section (just before the start of the next session plan). This little form gives you a place to write down the materials you'll need, too—since they depend on the options you've chosen.

(4) *Get your stuff together.* Gather your materials; photocopy any Repro Resources (reproducible student sheets) you've decided to use. And . . . you're ready!

The Custom Curriculum Challenge

Your kids are fortunate to have you as their leader. You see them not as a bunch of generic teenagers, but as real, live, unique kids. You care whether you really connect with them. That's why you're willing to take a few extra minutes to tailor your meetings to fit.

It's a challenge to work with real, live kids, isn't it? We think you deserve a standing ovation for taking that challenge. And we pray that **Custom Curriculum** helps you shape sessions that shape lives for Jesus Christ and His kingdom.

—*The Editors*

Talking to High Schoolers about Habits

by Fran and Jill Sciacca

Spiders spin webs by instinct, not by habit. It's part of their chromosomal chemistry. What's most amazing is that each web a spider spins is exactly the same! That means you'll never see a book called *One Hundred Creative Webs* at a bug bookstore. You'll also never hear of a vocational school for web-challenged spiders seeking a heroic spot in the Arachnid Hall of Fame!

There's a tremendous difference between instinct and habit. Instincts "happen" because they are programmed into a creature as it comes to life. Habits, on the other hand, are slowly cultivated. They grow out of *choices* concerning conscious behavior. Interestingly, however, by the time they become habits, they *appear* instinctual. That's because *habits are behaviors about which we no longer make choices.* In fact, we don't think much about them at all until they are pointed out to us by other people or by our circumstances. Habits pretty much operate subconsciously until someone or something brings them to our attention—for good or for ill.

A habit is different from an instinct in a second significant way. Habits can be started, stopped, and altered—three luxuries not available to instincts. Spiders can't redesign their web pattern unless their genetic map changes. Habits, on the other hand, can be recognized, identified, and cultivated or terminated. There is hope for stopping bad habits. A habit, though deeply imbedded, is not necessarily permanent. This is particularly true for those who possess the Spirit of God. God is the one who includes the following statements in His Word:

"See, I am doing a new thing! Now it springs up; do you not perceive it? I am making a way in the desert and streams in the wasteland" (Isaiah 43:19).

"Therefore, if anyone is in Christ, he is a new creation; the old has gone, the new has come!" (II Corinthians 5:17).

"I have been crucified with Christ and I no longer live, but Christ lives in me. The life I live in the body, I live by faith in the Son of God, who loved me and gave himself for me" (Galatians 2:20).

As you work through *Can't Help It?* rest assured that the God who changed water into wine can also break the habits of those He made in His image! Make it your goal to enlighten and enable your group members to see the greatness and power of God in all things.

The subject of habits can be both personal and emotional. Be careful not to tease anyone about any habit (major or minor) that you may have noticed. Steer conversations away from exposing one another's bad habits. Create an atmosphere of acceptance in your group from the very beginning of the study.

We Are What We Choose

Keep in mind that today's young people are growing up in an age when casting blame is more common than admitting guilt. From presidents to parents, kids hear why people shouldn't be held responsible for their choices. Blame lies elsewhere. Young people have been taught that *they* can be excused from bad behavior too. Abusive parents, insensitive teachers, and a culture that is deaf to their needs and pains are really to blame for all of their anger, lostness, and despair. It's no secret that many teens are broken and devastated from their life circumstances. But, in the words of our own junior high son, "Dad, the fact that Mike has no father may help explain *why* he treats me like this, but it's not fair that it should *excuse* it!" This comment came one night in frustration after an angry boy at school had relentlessly attacked our son all day. My son's insights were accurate and his statement was true!

Habits always begin as choices. These are conscious, deliberate choices—whether they involve biting fingernails or experimenting with drugs. But, over time, the *conscious* portion diminishes and we're left with mere behavior. An excellent example of this process is found in the Book of Jeremiah. In reprimanding the Jews of Judah, the prophet speaks of them as first *refusing* to admit their guilt, and then eventually becoming shameless and incapable of even feeling guilty (see Jeremiah 3:3; 6:15). What began as a choice ended as a habit. Ownership of habits is an important starting place because it makes me a participant rather than merely a spectator in the process.

We Are What We Worship

Habits are also assimilated or broken by what we value most. It is an indisputable principle of God's Word that people *become* what they worship. The prophet Jeremiah stung the Jews of Judah with this barb of truth: "This is what the Lord says: 'What fault did your fathers find in me, that they strayed so far from me? They followed worthless idols and became worthless themselves' " (Jeremiah 2:5).

Many people don't realize the intense connection between what we value and how we act. We live our lives based on what's important to us, and because what we repeatedly do eventually becomes habitual, our values will shape our habits. If I say that I am a Christian, but value the message and music of secular groups that mock biblical truths, I will eventually develop the habits and lifestyle associated with the message of their music—and not those of Jesus Christ. This is as true of adults as it is of teens!

What I believe about money will dictate my work habits and my ethics regarding how to obtain wealth. My convictions about pleasure will control my sexual behaviors, both private and shared. The list goes on. As you move through *Can't Help It?* make sure your group members see the bigger picture. Who or what has first place in their lives will quietly and consistently control the habits that govern all that they do.

We Are Who We Hang With

A final insight about habits has to do with the impact of others upon us. Our lives will be shaped by the people we hang with. Whether it's smoking cigarettes or memorizing Scripture, evangelism or entertainment, most of the kids who sit before you are doing things that "significant others" in their lives do. This is a two-edged sword that can cut either way. Solomon, a man who knew a great deal about habits—good and bad—captured this truth succinctly when he wrote "He who walks with the wise grows wise, but a companion of fools suffers harm" (Proverbs 13:20).

In Scripture, the fool and the wise person are differentiated by the things that characterize their lives—their habits. The Book of Proverbs carefully and colorfully portrays the fool as acting one way and the wise person as acting another way. Those distinguishing characteristics are transferable and reproducible. Help your kids see the serious impact that their associations have on their habits. Birds of a feather don't just "flock together"; they tend to "fly" the same way too!

Too often, we focus on isolating and changing bad habits, with no basic understanding of what habits really are or where they come from. Habits are much more than mere behaviors. *They are a reflection of my character, what I'm living for, and who I'm traveling with.* Habits are indicators, at a very basic level, of *who I am*. A more serious truth is that habits also contribute, to a great degree, to who I become.

As you work through the five sessions of *Can't Help It?* it's our prayer that you will do so with an appreciation of the role habits play in our lives, and an enthusiastic awareness of the significance of your leading teens through this material. Make a *habit* of reminding yourself that what you're doing really matters—for eternity!

Fran and Jill Sciacca have been involved with youth ministry for nearly two decades. Fran is a high school teacher. Jill has a degree in journalism and sociology and is a full-time homemaker and free-lance writer/editor. She has written for Discipleship Journal *and* Decision *magazine and has served on the editorial team for the* Youth Bible (Word). *Fran and Jill coauthored* Lifelines (Zondervan), *an award-winning Bible study series for high schoolers. Fran is the author of the best-selling Bible study,* To Walk and Not Grow Weary (NavPress), *as well as* Generation at Risk (Moody), *and* Wounded Saints (Baker).

The images on these two pages are designed to help you promote this course within your church and community. Feel free to photocopy anything here and adapt it to fit your publicity needs. The stuff on this page could be used as a flier that you send or hand out to kids—or as a bulletin insert. The stuff on the next page could be used to add visual interest to newsletters, calendars, bulletin boards, or other promotions. Be creative and have fun!

Are You Carrying Some Baggage That You'd Like to Get Rid Of?

Do you have any habits in your life that you can't seem to stop? You're not alone. Join us as we begin a very special new series called *Can't Help It?* The results could be life-changing.

Who:

When:

Where:

Questions? Call:

Can't Help It?

Can't Help It?

How do you get rid of habits?

(Write your own ideas in the thought balloons.)

What is "It"?

Need someone to talk to?

It's OK to Struggle

YOUR GOALS FOR THIS SESSION:

Choose one or more

☐ To help kids recognize what habits are.

☐ To help kids understand that everybody struggles with habits.

☐ To help kids complete a personal inventory regarding their habits.

☐ Other _____

_____

Your Bible Base:

1 Corinthians 6:9, 10, 12

What's a Habit?

(Needed: Copies of Repro Resource 1, pencils)

Welcome group members as they arrive. If your kids are aware of the topic of this study, they may be a little apprehensive about this first meeting. Do your best to make them feel at ease by creating a relaxed atmosphere. Tell a few jokes. Take a few minutes to ask about any good movies or TV shows your group members have seen recently. Gradually ease into the material.

To begin the session, hand out copies of "A Habit Is . . ." (Repro Resource 1) and pencils. Give kids a few minutes to complete the sheet. When everyone is finished, ask volunteers to share their responses. Then go through the list of definitions again, this time asking group members to make personal applications.

For the first definition, ask: **Can you think of a pattern of behavior in your own life that's become almost involuntary because you've repeated it so often? If so, what is it?** Encourage kids to share some "harmless" patterns of behavior. For instance, some kids may have a certain "washing pattern" in the shower that they regularly follow (for example, face first, then hair, then the left armpit, and so on).

For the second definition, say: **Name a particular practice or custom that irritates you or that you don't understand.** For example, who decided that pressing your lips against someone else's lips is a way to show romantic feelings?

For the third definition, ask: **What would you say is a dominant characteristic or tendency of yours?** Ask volunteers to respond, but don't force anyone to answer who doesn't want to. Be prepared to share what you think is one of your dominant characteristics or tendencies.

For the fourth definition, ask group members to silently consider an addiction that they're familiar with to see how it fits the definition of a habit.

Good, Bad, or Neither?

Read again the definition at the bottom of Repro Resource 1: "A habit is something we do the same way every time or something we do without thinking."

Then ask: **Based on this definition, would you say a habit is good, bad, or neither? Explain.** It's likely that your group members will say that some habits are good, some are bad, and some are neither.

Say: **A good habit might be defined as something useful you do without thinking because you've become so good at it that you don't *have* to think about it.** Ask kids to name some examples of good habits. These examples might include remembering people's names and saying "please" and "thank you."

Say: **A bad habit might be defined as something negative or destructive you do without thinking—perhaps as a knee-jerk reaction.** Ask group members to list some examples of bad habits. Such examples might include swearing and being sarcastic.

Say: **Habits that are neither good or bad might involve things you do naturally, without ever having "learned" to do them.** Ask kids to list some examples of habits that are neither good or bad. Examples might include things as basic as breathing and rubbing your hands together when they're cold.

Have group members consider the examples they came up with for good and bad habits. Then ask: **What are some things you wish you could do without thinking? Why?** (Someone might say that he wishes it were natural for him to start conversations with strangers because he'd like to be more friendly.) Volunteers may share their responses if they like, but you're really just asking group members to silently consider the question.

Then ask: **What are some things you wish *didn't* come so naturally for you? Why?** (Someone might say that she wishes sarcasm didn't come so naturally to her because she has a tendency to hurt others with her words.)

At this point in the session, give group members an opportunity to ask any questions or share any insights they have about habits. Be prepared to address (if not answer) any questions and respond to any insights your group members may offer. Then move on to the next section.

O P T I O N S

EXTRA ACTION

LARGE GROUP

HEARD IT ALL BEFORE

LITTLE BIBLE BACKGROUND

MOSTLY GUYS

URBAN

STEP 3

Establishing Ground Rules

(Needed: Copies of Repro Resource 2, pencils)

OPTIONS

SMALL GROUP

MOSTLY GIRLS

SHORT MEETING TIME

JR.HIGH HIGH SCHOOL COMBINED

EXTRA CHALLENGE

Point out that in the weeks ahead, your group members will be helping each other deal with difficult personal problems that stem from habits. Explain that having the right attitude as a group will go a long way toward making the process easier.

Hand out copies of "Can We Talk?" (Repro Resource 2). Give group members a few minutes to read through the sheet. When everyone is finished, go through the questions as a group, allowing kids to comment on any of them they wish to. Use the following questions as needed to guide your discussion of the sheet.

No Fluff

• *Are you willing to make this a "no-fluff zone"?* Ask: **What is a no-fluff zone? Why is it important for us not to allow fluff—unimportant, "surfacy" discussion—in our meetings? How can we create a no-fluff zone for our meetings?**

• *Will you work with us to help us stay on track?* Ask: **What are some of the dangers of getting off track in our discussions? What strategies can we use to make sure we stay focused on the topic at hand?**

Support

• *Are you willing to support the rest of us by listening when we talk?* Ask: **What are some ways that we can we let each other know that we're listening?**

• *Are you willing to support the rest of us by asking questions to help us clarify what we mean?* Ask: **What kinds of questions could you ask to get a clearer understanding of what someone is talking about?**

• *Are you willing to support the rest of us by praying for us?* Ask: **Would you be willing to commit to a regular prayer time—perhaps daily or weekly—in which you prayed for the rest of us in this group?**

• *Are you willing to support the rest of us by encouraging us?* Ask: **What could someone in this group say to you that would encourage you? What encouragement could you give others?**

Confidentiality

• *Are you willing to keep what you hear in this group private?* Ask: **Why is confidentiality so important in this group?**

• *Will you respect the right of each person in this group to tell his or her own story when he or she is ready?* Ask: **Why is it so important that we not force anyone to share who isn't comfortable doing so?**

Protection

• *If you become convinced that one of us is in serious danger, are you willing to stay with that person until the two of you can find an adult you both trust to help?* Ask: **How will you decide whether or not someone is in "serious danger"?**

Other

• *Are there any other agreements that you think would make this a safe place to be honest about your life? If so, write them in the space below.* Allow several minutes for group members to share what they came up with.

Encourage group members to keep Repro Resource 2 handy throughout the rest of this series as a reminder of the perimeters you've set for the group.

STEP

4

Masters and Servants

(Needed: Bibles, copies of Repro Resource 3, pencils)

Have someone read aloud I Corinthians 6:12. Then ask: **What do you think it means to be "mastered" by something?** (Allowing something to have control over you.)

How might a person become mastered by something? (Perhaps mastery occurs when a person becomes so involved in a practice or habit that he or she seemingly has no choice in whether or not he or she continues that practice or habit.)

What's the problem with allowing yourself to be mastered by something? (As Christians, the only Master we should have is the Lord.)

Have someone read aloud I Corinthians 6:9, 10. Then ask: **Based on these verses, what are some things that you believe could master a person?** (Sexual immorality—including adultery, prostitution, and homosexual practice; idolatry; thievery; greed; drinking; slander; and being deceitful.)

Are there some other things you see in the world around you that you would add to this list of potential "masters"? If

OPTIONS

LARGE GROUP

HEARD IT ALL BEFORE

LITTLE BIBLE BACKGROUND

FELLOWSHIP & WORSHIP

MOSTLY GIRLS

MOSTLY GUYS

EXTRA FUN

MEDIA

JR. HIGH HIGH SCHOOL COMBINED

EXTRA CHALLENGE

so, what are they? Encourage several group members to offer their input.

Then ask: **Have you ever been mastered by anything—perhaps a substance, a behavior, a relationship, an attitude, a mood, or an emotion?** Emphasize that you're merely looking for a yes-or-no answer here. Do *not* ask for details regarding what kinds of things mastered your group members.

Then hand out copies of "Is It a Problem?" (Repro Resource 3). Give group members a few minutes to complete the sheet. Emphasize that this sheet is designed to allow group members to honestly (and privately) examine habits in their lives; no one will be asked to share his or her responses.

Afterward, ask: **Without feeling like you have to get specific with us, what do your answers tell you about "It"?** Encourage kids to respond, but don't force anyone to share.

Would you feel comfortable or safe sharing your struggles with "It" with us in this group? Why or why not? If not, what would it take to make you feel comfortable about sharing? Emphasize that you're not asking group members to share right now; you're just trying to find out how comfortable they are with the group.

As you wrap up the session, encourage group members to consider ways to improve the group, to make it more conducive to sharing. Close the session in prayer, thanking God for the courage and honesty your group members displayed in identifying habits that they need to address. Ask God to help your group members remain open to sharing their habits with the group in the weeks to come.

A Habit Is . . .

Brainstorm a list of items that fit the following definitions of the word habit.
Some examples are provided for you to get you started.

hab-it *n.*

*1. an acquired pattern of behavior that has become almost
involuntary as a result of frequent repetition*
• For example, some people have a habit of brushing their
teeth according to a certain pattern.

*2. a particular practice,
custom, or usage*
• For example, the habit of
shaking hands is a customary
greeting in some parts of the world.

3. a dominant or regular characteristic or tendency
• For example, some people have a habit of criticizing others at every opportunity.

4. addiction
• For example, some people have a drug habit that
causes them to spend most of their time either getting high
or thinking about getting high.

[Definitions are adapted from The Random House Webster's College Dictionary, © 1991.]

A habit **is something** we **do**
the **same way every** time
or something We do
without thinking.

CAN WE TALK?

If we're really going to help each other deal with difficult habits, there are some agreements we need to make.

NO FLUFF

• Are you willing to make this a "no-fluff zone"?

• Will you work with us to help us stay on track?

SUPPORT

• Are you willing to support the rest of us by listening when we talk?

• Are you willing to support the rest of us by asking questions to help us clarify what we mean?

• Are you willing to support the rest of us by praying for us?

• Are you willing to support the rest of us by encouraging us?

CONFIDENTIALITY

• Are you willing to keep what you hear in this group private?

• Will you respect the right of each person in this group to tell his or her own story when he or she is ready?

PROTECTION

• If you become convinced that one of us is in serious danger, are you willing to stay with that person until the two of you can find an adult you both trust to help?

OTHER

• Are there any other agreements that you think would make this a safe place to be honest about your life? If so, write them in the space below.

I want this to be a safe place. I agree that it will be a no-fluff zone. I promise to support the rest of the members of this group. I promise to maintain confidentiality regarding our discussions. I promise to protect the other people in this group to the best of my ability.

_____   _____

(your name)   (date)

IS IT A PROBLEM?

1. Think of a habit that was, is, or could be a problem for you. We'll call this habit **IT**. **IT** could be a substance, a behavior, a relationship, an attitude, a mood, or an emotion.

2. You won't be asked to identify **IT** out loud, but at least write **IT** or draw a symbol for **IT** in the space below. No one else will see what you write, so be honest with yourself in identifying **IT**.

3. Answer each of the following questions about **IT** by circling the appropriate response. Be honest.

• Does **IT** express true love for others?	Never	Sometimes	Always
• Do I do **IT** in secret?	Never	Sometimes	Always
• Do I do **IT** to control the way people see me?	Never	Sometimes	Always
• Would I be embarrassed or upset if **IT** were out in the open?	Never	Sometimes	Always
• Does **IT** cause trouble with people I care about?	Never	Sometimes	Always
• Do I do **IT** in the name of Christ?	Never	Sometimes	Always
• Do I do **IT** to numb bad feelings?	Never	Sometimes	Always
• Does **IT** build up others?	Never	Sometimes	Always
• Do I tell myself that I'm not going to do **IT** anymore?	Never	Sometimes	Always
• Does **IT** build me up?	Never	Sometimes	Always
• Do I suspect that **IT** may be a problem?	Never	Sometimes	Always
• Do I lie about **IT**?	Never	Sometimes	Always

Step 1

Order a "How Are You Feeling Today?" chart from Hazelden (15251 Pleasant Valley Road, P.O. Box 176, Center City, MN 55012, or call 1-800-328-9000). This cleverly illustrated chart displays thirty different emotions. As an opening activity for this and subsequent meetings, have your group members look over the chart, determine how they are feeling at that specific moment, and write their names beside the appropriate emotion. In lieu of ordering the poster, post a sheet of newsprint, scatter some markers around, and let kids draw themselves in a way that would reflect their current mood.

Step 2

Young people aren't likely to open up immediately and begin to discuss their own bad habits. For a less threatening option, have kids work in groups to design "Bad Habit Man," a cartoon character who personifies every bad habit they can think of. As much as possible, the character's habits should be illustrated. When it's not possible to do so, however, kids may describe habits in a list beneath the illustration. When groups finish, let each one show its version of Bad Habit Man and read any necessary descriptions.

Step 1

In a large group, someone who has serious problems may be able to remain "on the fringe" of the discussion and not have to open up. But in a small group, it's hard to remain silent without calling attention to oneself. To help kids feel more comfortable about approaching the topic of habits, begin by discussing the habits *of the group.* Do you almost always play games or sing before beginning the session? Are the chairs arranged the same way from week to week? Do people sit in the same places? Are some people usually talkative while others keep quiet? Discuss your group's habits. Is each one good or bad? Do some of them need to be changed? Do any need to be eliminated? Help kids see that *discussing* habits is a neutral activity. The habits themselves might be good or bad, but there can be no harm in taking an objective look at them. Lead in to a discussion of your kids' habits.

Step 3

As you establish ground rules, help your kids feel as nonthreatened as possible. One way to do this is to post a copy of Repro Resource 2 in the meeting area. If possible, enlarge it to poster size. Number the headings as follows: (1) No Fluff; (2) Support; (3) Confidentiality; (4) Protection; and (5) Other. Explain that any time someone begins to encroach on a person's rights in the group, the offended person may stop the discussion and challenge the other person. For example, if someone is trying to share a sensitive story and someone else is talking or making fun, the first person should say, "I think you're in violation of Rule #2." People in a small group will find it extremely hard to open up if they aren't convinced of the support and confidentiality of others in the group.

Step 2

Hand out paper and pencils. Instruct each person to list every personal habit he or she can think of. Explain that it doesn't matter how major or how insignificant a habit seems; kids should just make their lists as long as possible. Collect the lists; then designate various areas of the room as "Good," "Bad," and "Neither." Read the items from your group members' lists at random; have kids stand in the section of the room that indicates their opinion of each habit. The large number of people in your group should allow for a wide diversity of opinion. Whenever people stand in different sections of the room, let representatives from each section explain why they chose that section instead of the other two. This should be done quickly, however. It is more important to cover a lot of different habits at this point than to get into an in-depth discussion.

Step 4

When you begin the session, divide the group into "Masters" and "Servants," so that each Master has four to six personal Servants. Throughout the session, give the Masters authority to command their Servants to do various things (within reason). Try to have some fun with this during the session. When you get to Step 4, let your Servants describe what they think of life under the control of a Master. After having a literal experience, kids should be in a better position to understand being "mastered" by some of their bad habits.

Step 2

Kids who think they've heard it all before may consider the differences between a good habit and a bad habit to be rather obvious. If this is true with your group, try to "blur the lines" between a good habit and a bad habit. Ask: **Would you say that reading the Bible is a good habit?** Probably most of your kids will say yes. If they do, ask: **What if a person was in the habit of reading one Bible chapter a day, as fast as he or she could, without really understanding—or even trying to understand—what he or she was reading? Would you still say it was a good habit? Why or why not?** Get a few responses. Use any other examples like this that you can think of.

Step 4

Spend some time exploring the ironic relationship between being free to do as one pleases and being mastered by something. Ask: **How might complete freedom—the belief that "everything is permissible"—lead a person into a situation in which he or she is mastered by something?** (Kids who feel free to drink or take drugs may find themselves mastered by an addiction. Kids who feel free to satisfy their sexual urges according to their own whims may find themselves mastered by compulsive sexual behavior.) **How is it possible to enjoy the freedom of the Christian life without becoming mastered by something?** Use Romans 6:5-7 to supplement your discussion.

Step 2

Add a biblical perspective to the topic of habits. Explain that after people become Christians, the habits they had previously can cause them serious problems until they are willing and able to change them. Read Galatians 5:16-21 aloud. As you read, emphasize each item in the list of acts of the sinful nature. Ask kids to consider if any of these things might be some of their current habits. Then continue the passage by reading Galatians 5:22-26. Point out that while we are sometimes not able to do away with our bad habits on our own, God is able to help us. His Spirit enters the life of a Christian and provides the power to eventually do away with the acts of the old, sinful nature. In their place we can discover genuine love, joy, peace, and all the rest of the things God has to offer. That's why we need to do what we can to work on the habits that impede our growth.

Step 4

People new to the Bible may be surprised at the context of the verses cited in the session (I Corinthians 6:9, 10, 12). Explain that Paul was writing to a messed-up church. Have someone read I Corinthians 5:1, 2 to find what the specific problem was. Not only was a man sleeping with "his father's wife" (probably his stepmother, which was forbidden), but the church was taking pride in being accepting of such behavior. Ask: **Can you think of ways that people sometimes get their thinking so twisted that they're actually proud of their bad habits?** (Some people think that they can drink a lot without being affected; others seem to take pride in their abrasive personalities; and so on.) Point out that sometimes this attitude is intentional. Other times, however, our thinking becomes twisted without our awareness. That's why it's important to take a close look at habits that seem to come naturally.

Step 1

When kids arrive, assign each person the name of a TV show. Hand out pencils and paper. Explain: **You need to find out the names of five other people's assigned TV shows. After you discover what a person's assigned show is, have the person write the name of the show on your sheet of paper and then sign his or her name next to it. The catch is that the person whose show you're trying to guess is not allowed to talk.** Allow several minutes for kids to pantomime and guess each other's shows. Award a prize to the first person who correctly guesses five shows. Afterward, say: **TV often gets a pretty bad rap. What's so bad about TV?** (Violent shows, bad language, sex, and so on.) If no one mentions it, suggest that TV can be habit-forming. Then ask kids to name some other things that can be habit-forming. After kids have offered several suggestions, explain that in the next few weeks you'll be examining the topic of habits.

Step 4

After your kids have identified an "It" in their lives that could be a potential problem, explain that the best thing to do with any problem is to give it to God. Emphasize that there are many ways He can help us with our problems, but we need to bring them to Him first. Have group members sing or listen to a recording of "Cast All My Cares upon You." Then encourage your kids to do that, to cast their cares upon the Lord. Allow a time for kids to pray silently; then close the session by praying aloud for your group members, asking God to help each person with his or her "It."

Step 3

Before you begin Step 4, ask your group members to name some things that might "master" girls their age—things that your group members' peers may struggle with. Hand out paper and art supplies. Ask your girls to draw representations of those mastering things. The representations may be anything from a personified character- ization to a symbolic swirl of colors. After a few minutes, have your girls display and explain their characterizations.

Step 4

Girls are often more open and willing to share with each other than guys are. If your girls agree to it, set them up in pairs, making sure that they're comfortable with their partners. Encourage them to share with their partners what their "It" is as identified on Repro Resource 3. Encourage partners to share their struggles; allow time for them to pray with each other. Afterward, ask if any of your girls feel better about their "It," just knowing that there's someone else who knows about it. Often, just talking about a problem brings relief. Encourage the partners to pray for each other throughout the series.

Step 2

When you start listing various habits in this step, begin by focusing exclusively on "guy habits." Have group members list every- thing they can think of that would apply to the category as you write their responses on the board. These don't have to be habits that apply specifically to *your* group of guys, but should apply to the male gender overall. Some such habits will probably be stereotypical: scratching and spitting, remote control surfing, acting tough (especially when girls are around), and so forth. But with time, group members will probably begin to share more personal habits: reluctance to show true feelings, resistance to crying, and so forth. After you make the list, go through each habit and rate it as good, bad, or neutral. By discussing the habits of guys as a whole, you take pressure off your *specific* group of guys, while still discussing the issue honestly.

Step 4

Close the session by starting a new habit. Create a completely new tradition that your guys can do at each meeting that will be positive and special to them. You might want to do something to facilitate the commitment group members agree to have toward one another on Repro Resource 2. For example, you might create a unique hand signal to communicate, "I'd like your full attention for the next few minutes." You might devise your own "manly" method of showing affection for one another (if hugs aren't masculine enough for your guys). It doesn't matter what your new habit is, as long as your guys are involved in creating it and committed to continuing it.

Step 1

Begin the session with a charades-like game. On individual slips of paper, write the names of famous people, past or present. Have each group member draw a name and begin to act as that person. All group members should do this simulta- neously, so that they are portraying their own person while trying to figure out everyone else's. They can attempt to guess each other's character at any time, as long as they stay in character themselves. When everyone has guessed correctly (or has given up), announce that you will play one more round. This time, however, write down the names of all of the kids present. Let group members attempt to portray each other. To do so, they will probably adopt each other's outward habits, which should lead in to the topic of the session.

Step 4

In connection with Repro Resource 3, give kids an opportunity to draw their habits as if they were actual characters. In other words, what does "It" look like? Explain that you don't want kids to indicate what the habit is, but only to transform "It" into some kind of character. Is "It" small or large? Is "It" enticing or mean? Is "It" a hairy habit? Does "It" have teeth? Is "It" aggressive or reclusive? If your kids simply cannot draw what they wish, let them make comparisons to existing characters. Perhaps their habit is much like the Tasmanian Devil, Bart Simpson, Wile E. Coyote, or any number of other charac- ters. Let all group members who are willing show the characters they drew.

Step 1

If you plan to work through this entire five-session series, you might want to consider subscribing to some of the periodicals that deal with coping with bad habits and addictions. Many resources can be recommended by The National Association for Christian Recovery, P.O. Box 11095 Whittier, CA 90603. The organization publishes a quarterly magazine called *Steps.* If you need help understanding the concepts in these sessions or finding additional material for kids who are interested, this would be an excellent starting point. Also ask around for other trustworthy local or national organizations that can help provide you with some materials to use throughout your study.

Step 4

Close the session by playing portions of songs by a variety of popular artists. The first "set" should include musicians such as Eric Clapton, Pete Townsend, Elton John, Aerosmith, and others you may know of who used to be addicted to drugs or drinking but now claim to be "clean." See if any of your kids can find the connection. Before you tell them what it is, play a second set of song portions by Jimi Hendrix, Janis Joplin, Nirvana (Kurt Cobain), Jim Morrison, and others who died young as a result of their "bad habits." This connection might be easier to make. Explain that even people in the excesses and depravity of rock and roll have seen the importance of getting rid of bad habits before those habits take permanent control of them.

Step 1

Replace Steps 1 and 2 with a shorter opener. As you begin the session—when you're making announcements or welcoming group members—display some kind of patterned behavior. Perhaps you might pace back and forth in front of the group, taking three steps to the left and then three steps to the right. Or perhaps you might begin every sentence with "You know . . ." It doesn't really matter what the patterned behavior is as long as you're consistent with it. See how long it takes kids to recognize what you're doing. Lead in to a discussion of habits. Ask: **What are some habits that you or people you know have? Would you say a habit is good, bad, or neither? Why?** Ask kids to list some things that they consider to be good habits and some things that they consider to be bad habits. Then move on to Step 3.

Step 3

Rather than having kids read through Repro Resource 2, allow them to establish their own guidelines for group discussion. Ask: **What would it take for you to feel comfortable about discussing your bad habits with the people in this group?** Some kids may say that they would need to be assured that what they say wouldn't be shared with anyone outside the group. Others may say that they would need to know that no one would laugh at or make fun of the things they share. Write group members' suggestions on the board as they're named. After you've compiled your list, ask group members to commit to following the guidelines on the board for the duration of this series.

Step 1

After you discuss the first definition on Repro Resource 1, ask volunteers to come to the front of the room one at a time to demonstrate and explain the usual patterns they follow when they do the following things: eat, get dressed, try to find something to watch on TV, do homework, get ready for bed, and so on. Be prepared to demonstrate some of your own patterns in these activities. After several volunteers have shared, move on to the second definition on Repro Resource 1.

Step 2

After reading again the definition at the bottom of Repro Resource 1 ("A habit is something we do the same way every time or something we do without thinking"), discuss some of the problems that can arise when we do things without thinking. Ask group members to consider possible results of doing certain things without thinking. For example, you might ask: **What might happen if you were to try to walk through some of the neighborhoods in your area at night without thinking? What might happen if you were to try to play basketball on an "A-level" court without thinking?** Add any other situations that you can think of.

Step 3

Some of your junior highers may not be mature enough to take seriously the agreements on Repro Resource 2. If so, split up your junior highers and high schoolers at this point. Give your high schoolers Repro Resource 2 to work through. Meanwhile, talk with your junior highers, asking them what things about a group setting might make it difficult for them to share and open up. Then ask them to come up with ideas for commitments that they can make to create a safe place to share. You might want to bring up the main points listed on Repro Resource 2: No Fluff, Support, Confidentiality, and Protection. Have them create a statement similar to the one on Repro Resource 2— one that is in their own words, which they will all copy and sign. When both groups are finished, bring them back together to make a mutual agreement, working together to create a safe zone.

Step 4

After reading 1 Corinthians 6:12, ask: **What is the difference between something that is "permissible" and something that is "beneficial"?** Allow for discussion; then make two lists, one of things that are permissible and one of things that are beneficial. After reading 1 Corinthians 6:9, 10, discuss the questions given in Step 4. Then read 1 Corinthians 6:11. Say: **It's true that no sinners will inherit the kingdom of God, but we're all sinners. So does that mean no one will get to heaven?** (Of course not.) **Why?** Remind your kids often of the Good News—and of the fact that there is both help and forgiveness for sinful habits and behaviors.

Step 3

After kids have agreed to the ground rules described in this step, ask: **With these commitments in mind, does anyone have anything to share that would make him or her more vulnerable to this group than ever before?** You might begin by sharing something about yourself to show what you're talking about. For example, you might say something like **I've been known to swear when I'm around other adults** or **I used to have an eating disorder that I'm over now, but that controlled me for a while.** Try to show kids that it's not only going to be OK to discuss personal things during these sessions, but that they should feel at ease to do so.

Step 4

If you determine from this first session that several of your group members may have problems more severe than they have let on in the past, you may ask some of them to form a support group to meet in addition to the regular youth group. You may know of resources that can help them. Or you may be equipped to put together something for them yourself. But if you need help, you can get some ideas from Confident Kids Support Groups, P.O. Box 11095, Whittier, CA 90604.

Date Used:

Approx.
Time _____

Step 1: What's a Habit?
o Extra Action
o Small Group
o Fellowship & Worship
o Extra Fun
o Media
o Short Meeting Time
o Urban
Things needed:

Step 2: Good, Bad, or Neither? _____
o Extra Action
o Large Group
o Heard It All Before
o Little Bible Background
o Mostly Guys
o Urban
Things needed:

Step 3: Establishing Ground Rules _____
o Small Group
o Mostly Girls
o Short Meeting Time
o Combined Junior High/High School
o Extra Challenge
Things needed:

Step 4: Masters and Servants _____
o Large Group
o Heard It All Before
o Little Bible Background
o Fellowship & Worship
o Mostly Girls
o Mostly Guys
o Extra Fun
o Media
o Combined Junior High/High School
o Extra Challenge
Things needed:

Why Do Habits Grow?

YOUR GOALS FOR THIS SESSION:

Choose one or more

☐ To help kids recognize how people get trapped in bad habits.

☐ To help kids understand the difference between "acting out" and "acting in" in response to habits.

☐ To help kids complete an honest self-examination regarding the habits in their lives.

☐ Other _____

_____

Your Bible Base:

Romans 7:14-25

Ad It Up

(Needed: Magazines, scissors)

To begin the session, have kids form pairs. Hand out magazines and scissors to each pair. Instruct the pairs to cut out advertisements in the magazines that appeal to or address people's habits. (If the pairs finish quickly, you might ask them to think of similar TV and radio commercials.) For instance, cigarette and alcohol ads certainly appeal to people's habits. Also, ads for nicotine patches and organizations like Alcoholics Anonymous address people's habits. Give the pairs a few minutes to work. When everyone is finished, ask each pair to display and explain its ads.

Afterward, instruct each pair to join up with another pair to form groups of four. Explain that each person should answer the following questions within his or her small group. Allow fifteen seconds for each person to answer each question. The questions are as follows:

• **Where do you fit in your family birth order? For instance, are you the firstborn child in your family? A middle child? The "baby" of the family? What's that like?**

• **Share an early secure memory.**

• **Share an early guilty or insecure memory.**

• **On a scale of one to ten, with one being "very easy" and ten being "very difficult," how hard is it for you to share about yourself? Explain.**

Give kids a few minutes to answer the questions in their small groups. When everyone is finished, ask the members of each group to talk about how smoothly the communication process went in their group.

Ask: **How comfortable did you feel sharing personal information with the other people in your group? Explain.**

How comfortable did you feel listening to others share personal information? Explain.

After you get a few responses, say: **You've practiced opening up in a small group setting, but what about in a large group setting? How easy or hard do you think it will be to share personal information with all of us regarding specific habits in your life? Explain.** Get as many responses as possible.

STEP

2

The Incredible Growing Habit

(Needed: Copies of Repro Resource 4, pencils)

O P T I O N S

EXTRA ACTION

LARGE GROUP

MOSTLY GIRLS

MEDIA

Hand out copies of "How Habits Grow" (Repro Resource 4) and pencils. Give group members a few minutes to read through the top half of the sheet and then answer the questions on the bottom half.

When everyone is finished, ask: **At what stage would you say "It" becomes a problem in a person's life?** Encourage several kids to offer their opinions. If there is disagreement among group members, stage a brief, impromptu debate on the topic. Then go through the last three questions on the sheet.

Ask: **Without feeling like you have to be too specific, what stage is "It" at in your life?** Encourage several group members to respond. Emphasize that you're not asking—nor will you ever ask—group members to identify "It"; you just want to discuss, in general terms, how prominent "It" is in your kids' lives.

Ask: **How is that different from six months ago?** Encourage group members to consider how much prominence "It" has gained in their lives—not only in terms of how much time kids spend doing "It," but also in terms of how much time they spend *thinking about* "It." After group members have responded, ask a couple of them why they think "It" has gained prominence in their lives in the past six months.

Ask: **How is that different from a year ago?** Encourage your group members to respond honestly.

Then ask: **If you'd known a year ago that "It" would be at the stage it is now in your life, would you have done anything differently? If so, what? If not, why not?** Encourage several group members to respond. Their responses should give you an idea of how they feel about "It."

OPTIONS

STEP 3

Avoiding the Trap

(Needed: Copies of Repro Resource 5, chalkboard and chalk or newsprint and marker)

You'll need to have a copy of "The Trap" (Repro Resource 5) to refer to as you lead the following discussion. Explain: **An organization called Turning Point came up with a series of pictures to illustrate how we can get trapped by a bad habit.**

Draw the first picture on Repro Resource 5 on the board. Say: **The first step is experimentation. At this point, a person finds that a little bit of "It" goes a long way toward making him or her feel good.** Point out that at this stage, the feelings associated with the habit remain high while the frequency (the number of times the habit is performed) remains relatively low.

What are some examples of things that can make people feel good for a while? (Drinking can produce a "buzz." Drugs can produce a high. Food can serve as a comfort.)

Draw the second picture on Repro Resource 5 on the board. Say: **The second step is doing "It" socially. At this point, the person allows "It" to become part of his or her social life. The person may even set up personal rules for when he or she thinks "It" is appropriate.** Point out that at this stage, the feelings associated with the habit remain high, but the frequency increases.

Say: **Let's say a person's "It" is drinking. Give some examples of what the person might do at Step 2.** (After experimenting with his or her first taste of alcohol, the person might start drinking with his or her friends at weekend parties. The person might then set rules for his or her drinking behavior, such as "I will drink only with people I know" or "I will drink no more than two beers at a party.")

Draw the third picture on Repro Resource 5 on the board. Say: **The third step is preoccupation with "It." At this point, the person begins to violate his or her own sense of right and wrong in order to take care of "It." The person may begin to blow off other important things for the sake of "It." Even if the person isn't doing "It," he or she is probably thinking about "It."** Point out that at this stage, the highs associated with the habit aren't as high as they were before, and the lows are lower. In other words, "It" fails to offer the same relief it used to. This leads to a higher frequency, because the person needs "It" more often to achieve the same results.

Ask: **Using the example we used for Step 2, what might a person with a drinking habit do at Step 3?** (The person may violate his or her own sense of right and wrong by drinking with people he or she doesn't know or by drinking alone. The person may begin to blow off things like school and church in order to drink. The person may think a lot about when he or she will be able to drink again. The person may find that he or she needs more and more alcohol to achieve the same high.)

Draw the fourth picture on Repro Resource 5 on the board. Say: **The fourth step is doing "It" to feel normal. At this point, "It" is not fun anymore. From this point on, the person is likely to suffer loss of dignity, broken relationships, and spiritual numbness as a result of "It."** Point out that at this stage, the feelings associated with the habit range from low to merely normal. The frequency remains high.

Ask: **What might a person with a drinking habit do at Step 4?** (The person may lose dignity as a result of drunken episodes. The person may lose some of his or her friends as a result of his or her drinking. The person's spiritual life may suffer. The person may start resorting to desperate measures in order to support his or her drinking habit.)

Hand out copies of Repro Resource 5 to your group members. Give them a few minutes to review the diagrams and then answer the questions at the bottom of the sheet. When everyone is finished, ask volunteers to share their responses.

STEP
4

Acting Out and Acting In

(Needed: Bibles)

Say: **Habits can be divided into two categories: those that involve "acting out" and those that involve "acting in." Examples of acting out might include smoking, drinking, sexual promiscuity, fighting, and overeating—actions that involve an outside substance or another person. Examples of acting in might include fantasizing, compulsive masturbation,**

O P T I O N S

LITTLE BIBLE BACKGROUND

MOSTLY GIRLS

MOSTLY GUYS

MEDIA

and nail biting—actions that involve only one's self. Ask group members to suggest other examples of acting out and acting in.

Then ask: **Whose actions would you say are easier to recognize: the person who acts out or the person who acts in? Explain.**

Who would you say is in greater danger: the person who acts out or the person who acts in? Explain.

Would you say that you're more likely to act out or act in? Why? Encourage several group members to respond to these questions.

Afterward, have someone read aloud Hebrews 4:13. Then ask: **How does it make you feel to know that nothing is hidden from God's sight?** Get a few responses.

Then ask group members to silently consider this question: **What things will be hardest for you to "give account" for to God? Why?**

STEP 5

I Know What I'm Supposed to Do

(Needed: Bibles)

Have someone read aloud Romans 7:14-25. Then use some or all of the following questions to supplement your discussion of the passage.

Ask: **How would you describe the overall tone of this passage? Explain.** (There seems to be a great deal of confusion and frustration on the part of the author. What he wants to do, he doesn't do; what he doesn't want to do, he does.)

Which phrase, sentence, or verse stands out to you most in this passage? Why?

Do you see yourself at all in this passage? If so, where? Explain.

What's the most difficult thing for you to accept in this passage? What makes it so tough for you to accept?

Compare Paul's words in Romans 7 with the following quote from Annie Dillard's *Teaching a Stone to Talk*:

"It can never be satisfied, the mind, never." Wallace Stevens wrote that, and in the long run he was right. The mind wants to live forever, or to learn a very good

reason why not. The mind wants the world to return its love, or its awareness; the mind wants to know all the world, and all eternity, and God. The mind's sidekick, however, will settle for two eggs over easy.

The dear, stupid body is as easily satisfied as a spaniel. And incredibly, the simple spaniel can lure the brawling mind to its dish. It is everlastingly funny that the proud, metaphysically ambitious, clamoring mind will hush if you give it an egg.

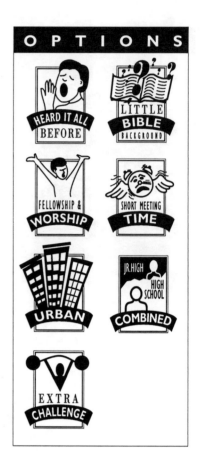

O P T I O N S

After reading the quote, ask: **What do you think of Annie Dillard's picture of "the dear, stupid body" and the "clamoring mind"? Explain.**
Can you think of a time when your body took over and overruled what you had already decided in your mind? Encourage a couple of group members to briefly share about such experiences. Then ask: **What did you learn from these situations?**
As you wrap up the session, give your group members an opportunity to share their thoughts regarding the things you've discussed. Use the following questions to guide your discussion.
• **What have you learned about yourself in this session?**
• **What have you learned about the rest of us in this session?**
• **Think about the "It" that you identified earlier. What have you done, are you doing, or would you like to do about "It"?**
• **What would you like the rest of us to pray for you?**
• **What would you like to say to God about the things we've talked about in this session?** Give kids an opportunity to pray silently or out loud (whichever they prefer); then close the session by praying for your group members according to the requests they listed for question 4.

HOW HABITS GROW

Habits follow a fairly predictable path as they grow. The process looks something like this:

Stage 1: Growing Fixation
I think about **IT** more and more.

Stage 2: Growing Inflexibility
I may not make it to class or make it home for dinner,
but I will definitely find time for **IT**.

Stage 3: Growing Tolerance
I need more of **IT** to be satisfied.

Stage 4: Growing Consequences
IT causes trouble in other parts of my life.

Identify a behavior, relationship, attitude, substance, mood, emotion, or any other habit that is a struggle for you. Let's call this habit **IT**. Identify **IT** with a word, phrase, or symbol in the space below. No one else will see what you write, so be honest with yourself in identifying **IT**.

Without feeling like you have to be too specific, what stage is **IT** at in your life?

How is that different from six months ago?

How is that different from a year ago?

THE TRAP

STEP 1: EXPERIMENTATION WITH IT

At this point, I find that a little bit of **IT** goes a long way toward making me feel good. For instance, food might make me feel better (at least for a while); driving fast might make me feel excited (at least for a while); and drinking might get me high.

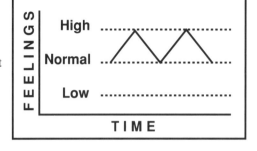

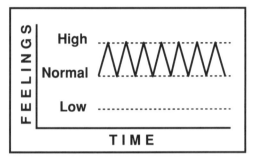

STEP 2: DOING IT SOCIALLY

At this point, **IT** becomes part of my social life. I may even set up personal rules for when I think **IT** is appropriate.

STEP 3: DAILY PREOCCUPATION WITH IT

At this point, I begin to violate my own sense of right and wrong in order to take care of **IT**. Over time, the highs don't get quite as high as they did before, while the lows get even lower. **IT** fails to give me the same relief **IT** used to. I blow off other important things for the sake of **IT**. Even if I don't do **IT**, I think about **IT**.

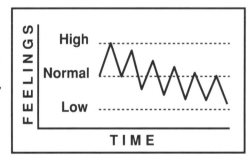

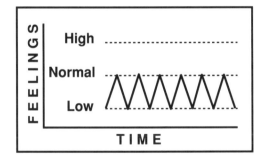

STEP 4: DOING IT TO FEEL NORMAL

At this point, I do **IT** just to feel "normal." From this point on, I'm likely to suffer loss of dignity, broken relationships, and spiritual numbness as a result of **IT**. **IT** is no fun anymore.

Does this sheet raise or answer any questions for you? If so, what are they?

What strikes you as the most interesting thing about these diagrams? Why?

Without naming any names, do you know someone who is at Step 4? If so, what seems to be **IT** for that person?

Again without naming names, do you know someone who is at Step 3? Step 2? Step 1? Describe some of these people.

How would you describe your own experience with the Trap?

Step 1
Begin the session by setting up your room as an aerobics class—the Bad Habits Aerobics Class. Get a leader to start everyone with some simple jumping jacks or running in place. After a few minutes, explain that as certain bad habits are called out, only the people with that specific bad habit have to exercise. Therefore, the more bad habits a person admits to, the harder he or she will work (symbolizing the way our bad habits can use up our energy). The "bad habits" you focus on should be nonthreatening at this point (nail biting, nose picking, drumming fingertips, talking too much, drinking milk directly from the carton, and so forth). After you wear everyone down a bit, start the session.

Step 2
As you discuss Repro Resource 4, have kids form groups to write and act out skits to demonstrate "how habits grow." But to prevent any embarrassment by getting "too close for comfort" for someone who might have a particular bad habit, use *good* habits for the skits. For example, in one skit, someone's habit of studying might get completely out of control. Other groups might deal with doing chores, being nice to brothers and sisters, practicing piano for a recital, or anything else that is positive. The same point can be made of how any single activity can become obsessive if we allow it to happen.

Step 1
Rather than having kids form small groups to discuss the questions in this step, let your entire group work together. Have kids assume the roles of trained psychiatrists whom you are paying to offer advice. Lie down somewhere in the room and begin to feed kids information along the lines of what you would like them to share with each other—early secure memories, early guilty memories, things associated with childhood that have become habits, and so forth. Explain that you have bad habits that you can't seem to get rid of. Let kids ask you questions to determine how best to help you. Afterward, ask: **How do you feel about discussing someone's personal history? How do you feel about discussing *your own* personal history? Is anyone willing to share an influential or important childhood memory with the rest of the group?** Continue the session as written from this point.

Step 3
After using drinking as an example for Repro Resource 5, come up with another example. Try to choose something as nonthreatening as possible—perhaps playing video games. Let kids choose one or more of the steps on Repro Resource 5. Ask them to convert the problem area into a human character. For example, in Step 1, the behavior might appear as a best friend ("Hey, let's go hang out. We can have a really cool time together"). By Step 4, however, the problem/character should be menacing ("Hey, creep, I'm your only friend, so you'll do what I say!"). One group member should play the role of the "victim." Try to have the victim converse with each of the behavior characters. If possible, he or she should ask questions and even challenge the authority of the characters wherever appropriate.

Step 2
Have kids form groups of ten. Explain that you will identify a number of areas that are problems for many teenagers. For each problem area you name, group members should give a shape to "It." Also, they should determine how severe a problem "It" is. For example, if they think "It" is a problem that affects everybody, then all of the people in the group should somehow be included in "Its" shape. If they don't think many people struggle with the problem, then "It" might be represented by only a person or two. Problem areas you might use include getting drunk, experimenting with drugs, going too far sexually, smoking, eating disorders, pornography, and so forth.

Step 3
After kids complete Repro Resource 5, select a name that isn't the name of anyone in the group. (Let's say it's Herbie.) Give Herbie a bad habit that many of your kids are likely to have to deal with. (Let's say it's drinking.) Then have your kids represent Herbie at different ages. The first person might be Herbie at 16, the next person Herbie at 17, and so forth. Have kids assume that Herbie does nothing to deal with his drinking habit. Ask them to project what will be happening to him when he reaches each age that is represented. (A large group can take Herbie throughout his lifetime.) Kids need not say much; a sentence will be fine ("At 32, Herbie is already experiencing shortness of breath and stomach problems"; "At 48, Herbie can no longer get car insurance because of his history of drunken driving"). Of course, your kids will have to do a lot of speculation and will probably deal with worst-case scenarios, which is fine. Explain that unresolved bad habits often result in "the worst" happening more often than people like to admit.

Step 1

Kids who are Sunday school and youth group "veterans" have probably done more magazine-cutting activities than they care to remember. So you might want to begin with a different opener. Have kids form pairs. Hand out paper and pencils to each pair. Give the members of each pair five minutes to list as many things as they can think of that cause (or help) a person to grow. Emphasize that you're not only talking about physical growth, but also spiritual growth, emotional growth, intellectual growth, and so on. For example, prayer and Bible study lead to spiritual growth; bouncing back from failure leads to emotional growth; reading books on different subjects leads to intellectual growth; and so on. If kids can successfully defend an item on the list as being "growth-inducing," the item counts. When time is up, have each pair share its list. Award prizes to the winning pair. Use this activity to introduce the topic of how habits grow.

Step 5

Have kids form pairs. Ask the members of each pair to imagine that they are advice columnists, whose job it is to dispense wisdom to troubled people. Read the following "letter" for your group members to respond to: **Dear Dr. Advice, I have a problem that's driving me nuts. Quite simply, I do not understand what I do. For what I want to do I do not do, but what I hate I do. I know it sounds crazy, but it's the truth. What can I do?** Emphasize that each pair must incorporate at least one relevant Bible passage in its response to the letter. After a few minutes, have each pair share what it came up with.

Step 4

Use discretion in discussing Hebrews 4:13 with kids who may not have a good understanding of *all* of God's attributes. To suddenly focus on His omniscience and judgment without considering His love as well can be frightening. Certainly nothing we do is hidden from God's sight, and that should be a sobering thought for anyone caught up in sinful behavior (which includes everyone from time to time). But explain to your group that this also means God sees things that we don't. We may see ourselves as worthless and helpless against our bad habits. But perhaps God sees an evil influence that needs to be removed, which He can do with no problem. God sees that we have value as individuals because He created us. He sees what we can be in all of our fullness, which we are incapable of comprehending. If you're not careful, you may add to your kids' problems by pointing out God's awareness of their behaviors and heaping guilt on top of an existing problem. But you also have the opportunity to affirm that God is the biggest (and most important) ally your kids will ever have in their battles to rid themselves of problem behavior.

Step 5

Romans 7:14-25 is a bleak passage if taken out of context. At the end of the session, explain that it serves as an introduction to Romans 8. Ask kids to read Romans 8 on their own during the coming week. If they are willing to go one step further, ask them also to write down every positive statement or promise they find in Romans 8. They should quickly see that while a life lived in one's own power seems pretty hopeless, a life devoted to God can be rich and full. With God's help—and *only* with His help—we can become "more than conquerors" (Romans 8:37) over any problem we face.

Step 1

Hand out a paper lunch bag to each group member. Have kids form teams. Give each team a supply of magazines, scissors, and tape. Instruct team members to cut out pictures or words that represent parts of them that they show to the world. Have them tape these pictures and words to the outside of their bags. Next, instruct them to cut out pictures or words that represent what's inside them, the parts of themselves that they don't let anyone else (or let only a very few people) see. Have them tape these pictures to the inside of their bags. When they've completed their bags, encourage them to share what they chose for the outsides of their bags with the other people on their team and explain why they chose what they did. Challenge, but don't force, them to share their "insides" as well. Then ask: **Why do you think it's easy or difficult for you to tell others your story?**

Step 5

As you wrap up the session, read Romans 7:14-25 again. Then say: **Isn't it encouraging to know that we're not alone in our struggles to do what's right? Even Paul, one of the greatest Christians who ever lived, struggled a lot with this.** Hand out paper and pencils. Have your group members write or draw a thank-you card to God for the help and strength He gives us to battle the "Its" of our lives. Ask kids to think about the specific ways that God can help them with a particular struggle. For instance, He gives us willpower to say no, provides good friends with whom we can share, gives us parents or counselors to give us advice, and so on. Encourage group members to ask God for specific help when they face "It" problems in their lives.

Step 2

Eating disorders—especially anorexia nervosa and bulimia—continue to be a real problem among adolescent girls. If no one in your group is suffering from an eating disorder, chances are good that at least some of your girls know someone who is. If there is someone in your group with an eating disorder, exercise extreme sensitivity in using this step. Ask your girls to think of someone they know who has an eating disorder. Talk about the stages presented in Step 2—why someone might develop the problem and how the person progresses from one stage to the next. Also discuss ways in which one can stop the process and get help along the way. End the discussion by praying for those who suffer from eating disorders.

Step 4

Read Hebrews 4:13 aloud. Then ask: **How does it make you feel when you hear that "everything is uncovered and laid bare" before God?** Get a few responses. Then ask: **Do you ever think about that when you're doing something "secretly"? Why or why not? How do you think knowing that could or should affect your behavior?**

Step 1

Some guys may be less influenced by print ads than by personal peer pressure. If you feel this is the case for your group members, do a roleplay instead of the ad-clipping exercise. Let one guy play the potential victim. The other guys should try to convince him that drinking floor wax is the new cool thing to do. These guys may be cunning and subtle, or they may outright lie to the victim. But their goal is to convince him to start the habit. See how well they do, and take note of the arguments that seem to get the victim's attention. Afterward, compare this to drinking or smoking. Ask: **If we know that something is harmful for us and can cause devastating tragedy later in life, why do we do it anyway?**

Step 4

Some of your guys may be able to provide very specific examples of "acting out" and "acting in" based on their own relationships. When guys start feeling pressure or emotional turmoil, they tend to punch walls, drive like maniacs, verbally abuse others who are smaller or weaker, exercise themselves into a frenzy, or any number of other things. Without naming names, have your group members make a list of all of the behaviors in each category ("acting out" and "acting in") that they have personally witnessed. By doing so, they will also be listing danger signals to watch for in their own lives.

Step 1

When you want kids to begin to share some of their memories, play "I've Got a Secret." Let kids take turns being the person with a secret. The secret can be anything from their past or present—a confession, a special talent, or anything else that others might find interesting. When the first volunteer has a secret in mind, the other group members will try to guess it by asking questions that can only be answered yes or no. As long as the person answers yes, the questioner may continue. But when the person answers no, the questioning moves on to the next person. If all kids have an opportunity to question a person and the secret is still not guessed, have the person reveal it to the group. Then the next volunteer takes a turn. If this game brings out a number of early secure memories and early guilty memories, you can move on from there. If it doesn't, you can pick up with those questions in Step 1.

Step 3

In connection with "The Trap" process on Repro Resource 5, have sets of volunteers play a game. One person should be blindfolded. Two or three others should be given prizes (dollar bills, candy, cassette tapes, etc.) or penalties (water guns, water balloons, shaving cream, Silly String, etc.). In each set of volunteers, at least one person should have a prize and at least one person should have a penalty. Other people might have additional prizes or penalties, or they might have nothing to offer. But it is the job of everyone to convince the blindfolded volunteer to choose him or her. This convincing can take the form of lying, threatening, begging, calling upon a long-standing friendship, or anything else that might work. When the blindfolded person chooses a person, he or she receives whatever the person has. Then call up the next set of volunteers.

MEDIA

Step 2

Have kids form teams. Instruct the members of each team to pretend that they're reporters for their school newspaper. The theme of this week's special edition is "Bad Habits on Campus." Have team members brainstorm ideas for stories. They should be sure to consider all aspects of coverage for the paper. Of course, they should give the most thought to what issues are *most* pressing—the front-page stories and any headlines they want to run. But they should also think about stories that might appear in the sports section. And how about the social pages? The personal ads? A special faculty section? If they were assigned to write an editorial for the editorial page, what would the headline be and what would the emphasis of the story? After a few minutes, have each team share what it came up with.

Step 4

If you've used the issue of drinking as a "sample" bad habit throughout this session, you might want to conclude by having kids watch the movie *Clean and Sober*, starring Michael Keaton as a man whose drinking "habit" became an addiction and got completely out of control before he determined to do something about it. For teenagers who haven't thought beyond the cool appearance of certain bad habits, this movie will show how much influence addictions begin to exert on a person, and how desperate people become to get rid of them. (If you are concerned with language in this film, you might want to look for someone who has taped it off a network broadcast and use the "edited for television" version.)

SHORT MEETING TIME

Step 1

Try a shorter opener. Hand out graph paper and pencils. Explain that you will call out different areas of your group members' lives. When you call out an area, group members should indicate on the graph paper how much they've grown or developed in that area in the past two or three years. You might call out areas like spiritual life, relationships with members of the opposite sex, relationships with friends, athletics, academics, relationships with parents or other family members, and so on. When you're finished, ask volunteers to share which areas they've grown the most in. Then move on to Step 2.

Step 5

Rather than using the Annie Dillard quote, wrap up the session with a discussion of Romans 7:14-25. After reading the passage, ask: **Why is it so difficult for us to do things that we want to do, but so easy to do things that we don't want to do? How do you feel when you find yourself doing something out of habit that you really don't want to do?** Read Romans 7:24, 25 again as an encouragement for your group members. Then close the session in prayer, thanking God that He is willing and able to "rescue" us from our habits.

URBAN

Step 1

Assign each person a habit at the beginning of the session that he or she must continue throughout the session. For instance, you might assign one person the habit of finger drumming. That person must drum his or her fingers on a desk or chair for the remainder of the session (much to the dismay of those around him or her). Periodically throughout the session, check to make sure that each person is continuing his or her habit. At the end of the session, see how many of the habits have become almost involuntary through repetition. Use this activity to make a point about how habits grow.

Step 5

Rather than using the Annie Dillard quote, spend some time getting some feedback from your group members regarding their feelings toward the struggle Paul describes in Romans 7:14-25. Ask: **On a scale of one to ten—with ten being the most—how closely do you identify with Paul's struggle? How do you feel when you want to do the right thing, but just can't seem to? Do your surroundings—the people you hang out with or the neighborhood in which you live—ever make it difficult for you to break a habit that you don't really want to continue? If so, how? What can be done about it?**

Step 3

Rather than using Repro Resource 5 as is, write the four steps on the board where everyone can see them. As a group, talk through each of the steps, making sure that your kids understand each one clearly. Then have group members form teams. Instruct each team to come up with a skit that shows the progression of these steps. The "It" may be anything—funny or serious—but each skit must include all four steps. After a few minutes, have each team present its skit.

Step 5

Parts of this step may fly right over the heads of your junior highers. After reading Romans 7:14-25 and making sure that everyone understands all of the "I do what I do not want to dos," have kids form teams. Give each team a piece of paper and a pencil. Instruct the teams to make two columns on their sheet—one labeled "Head" and the other labeled "Body." Under the Head column, have them list as many things as they can think of that they know they should do. Under the Body column, have them list as many things as they can think of that "get in the way of their head" and cause them to do things that they know they shouldn't. After a few minutes, have each team share its lists.

Step 3

For each step of "The Trap" described on Repro Resource 5, have group members try to think of relevant Scripture passages that would apply. Draw three columns on the board. The first column should contain the four steps of "The Trap." The second column should contain any biblical examples of each specific problem area or warnings about it. The third column should contain scriptural solutions or God's promises for help. Let group members work together to fill out as much as they can from memory. If there are any sections that they don't complete during the session, ask them to keep thinking (and possibly do a little research) during the week to see what they can come up with by the next meeting.

Step 5

You can have long and well-documented talks about the effects of bad habits and addictions without having much result on a lot of your group members. Sometimes kids need to see for themselves what can happen if their bad habits become addictive. So you might want to plan a group trip to an Alcoholics Anonymous or Alateen meeting. You can call the local Alcoholics Anonymous people in your area and ask for information about "open meetings" where everyone is welcome. Let your group members listen to some first-person stories and meet people who will be completely honest about what a "bad habit" can do.

3 We're in This Together

YOUR GOALS FOR THIS SESSION:

Choose one or more

☐ To help kids recognize that they can trust each other in the group setting.

☐ To help kids understand what addiction is.

☐ To help kids complete a Johari Window.

☐ Other _____
_____

Your Bible Base:

II Corinthians 4:1-11
James 5:16

Tuning Up

(Needed: Copies of Repro Resource 6, prizes [optional])

Have group members who were born on an odd-numbered day move to one side of the room while group members who were born on an even-numbered day move to the other side of the room. Explain that the two groups will be competing in a fast-paced variation of "Name That Tune."

Give the first group fifteen seconds to think of a song that refers to a woman, either by name or by gender (examples might include "Gloria" or "When a Man Loves a Woman"). The group must then sing at least one line from the song. When the first group finishes, the second group will then have fifteen seconds to think of and sing a line from another song that refers to a woman. Continue back and forth until one group can't think of another song. At that point, the other group gets a point.

Play several rounds in this manner, using different categories for each round. Other categories you might use include songs that refer to a man, songs that mention a body of water, and songs that have the word "love" in the title. Feel free to add other categories as you desire. However, your final category should be songs that refer to addiction.

The team with the most points at the end of the game is the winner. (You might want to consider awarding prizes to members of the winning team.)

After the game, have kids remain in their groups to discuss the following questions:

- **How do habits grow?**
- **What comments or questions regarding habits have you thought of since the last session?**
- **If someone asked you to describe an addiction, what would you say?**

After a few minutes, have a spokesperson from each group report on his or her group's responses.

Hand out copies of "The Invitation" (Repro Resource 6). Give group members a few minutes to read through the sheet.

When everyone is finished, ask: **Which things on this invitation stand out to you? Why?**

Do any of the items listed in the box seem familiar to you? Without getting too specific, how many of these items would you say are a problem for you?

Would you be interested in joining a group like the one described on the sheet? If so, why? If not, why not? Which things about the group appeal to you? Which things turn you off?

Encourage several kids to respond. Then spend some time comparing the group described on Repro Resource 6 with your group.

STEP 2

Run Away, Come Closer

(Needed: Copies of Repro Resource 7, chalkboard and chalk or newsprint and marker)

Say: **In his book *Addiction and Grace,* Gerald May describes two different kinds of addictions. He calls them "attraction addictions" and "aversion addictions."**

Hand out copies of "Attractions/Aversions" (Repro Resource 7). Refer group members first to the "Attractions" side of the sheet. Explain: **Attraction addictions are habits we develop because they make us feel good.** Give group members a minute or two to read through the list of attractions.

Discuss as a group some of the less obvious attraction addictions on the sheet. For example, you might ask questions like the following: **How might anger be an attraction to some people? How might someone become addicted to self-improvement? What is it about calendars that might be an attraction to some people?** Give group members an opportunity to identify some of the other attractions on the sheet that seem odd to them.

After you've discussed "Attractions," move on to the "Aversions" side of the sheet. Explain: **Aversion addictions are habits that express fears or dislikes.** Give group members a minute or two to read through the list of aversions.

Discuss as a group some of the less obvious aversion addictions on the sheet. For example, you might ask questions like the following: **Why might someone have an aversion to people who are competent? How might someone with an aversion to intimacy display that habit in his or her life?** Give group members an opportunity to identify some of the other aversions on the sheet that seem odd to them.

Write the following definition of *addiction* on the board:

OPTIONS

EXTRA ACTION
SMALL GROUP
LARGE GROUP
MOSTLY GIRLS
MOSTLY GUYS
SHORT MEETING TIME
URBAN
EXTRA CHALLENGE

"Dependence on or commitment to a habit, practice, or habit-forming substance to the extent that its cessation (ceasing) causes trauma (shock or extreme distress)." Then ask: **Based on this definition, how do you feel about using the word "addiction" to describe some of the things on these lists? Do you think addiction is too strong a word? Why or why not?** Encourage several group members to offer their opinions.

Then ask: **Could any of your past or present habits be called addictions? Do you see a potential for any current habits to become an addiction?** Emphasize that you're not asking kids to respond out loud to these questions; instead, you're asking them to answer the questions *honestly* to themselves. Encourage kids to review the lists on Repro Resource 7 as they consider the questions.

STEP 3

Hard Pressed

(Needed: Bibles)

Before you begin the Bible study, give group members an opportunity to respond to the information you covered in Steps 1 and 2. Use the following questions to get some feedback from your kids.

• **How do you feel about what we've talked about so far?**

• **On a scale of one to ten—with one being "very uncomfortable" and ten being "very comfortable"—how comfortable would you say you are talking about addictions? Explain.**

• **What are your feelings about the attractions and aversions listed on the addictions sheet? Explain.**

Give group members a few minutes to share their concerns and comments. Try to respond to as many of them as possible.

Have someone read aloud II Corinthians 4:1-11. Then ask: **How might you apply some of the principles in this passage to our study of habits and addictions?** Get a few responses.

Second Corinthians 4:2 talks about renouncing secret and shameful ways. What do you think that means? (The verse refers to maintaining integrity in the sight of God.)

It's one thing to *renounce* secret and shameful ways—to say, "I'm through with those things"; it's quite another thing to actually *end* such behavior. Why do you suppose ending secret and shameful behavior is difficult? Get several responses.

What do you think Paul is referring to in verse 7 when he talks about the "jars of clay"? (He's talking about human frailty.)

How do verses 8 and 9 make you feel? Why? (For some people, these verses might seem discouraging because they describe the persecution and confusion that all of us face. For others, these verses may offer hope because they suggest that no matter what obstacles and opposition we face, we can survive and prosper.)

How might you apply the principles in this passage to a specific habit with which you've struggled? You might begin the discussion by sharing a habit of your own that you could apply these principles to. Then encourage several group members to share.

Have someone read aloud James 5:16. Then ask: **How do you think this verse applies to our group?** Ideally, your group members will recognize the importance of being open with each other in the group setting concerning their habits and addictions.

Ask: **Why is it important for us to confess our sins to and pray for each other?** Get several responses.

STEP
4

A Window View

(Needed: Paper, pencils, chalkboard and chalk or newsprint and marker)

Explain: **In the 1950s, a diagram was developed to help us understand ourselves and each other. This diagram is called a Johari Window.** Distribute paper and pencils. Encourage kids to copy the diagram on their sheets as you draw it on the board.

Draw a large square on the board. Above the top line of the square, write the word "Myself." Along the left side of the square, write the word "Others." Draw a vertical line down the middle of the square, dividing the square in half. Then draw a horizontal line across the middle of the square, dividing the square into four equal sections.

In the top left section, write the word "Open." In the top right section, write the word "Secret." Explain: **The top panes in the window represent what I can see about me. Things in the "Open" window can be seen by me as well as by others. For instance, we can all see that I am . . .** (describe some obvious physical characteristics about yourself). Have group members suggest some other examples of things that might be in a person's "Open" window.

OPTIONS

Things in the "Secret" window can be seen by me, but not by others. For instance, you might be surprised to learn that . . . (reveal a secret about yourself that you're comfortable sharing). Have group members suggest some other examples of things that might be in a person's "Secret" window.

Then say: **We all have things in our "Secret" window—habits and addictions, for instance—that we have to decide whether we want to share with others or not. I just revealed to you something in my "Secret" window. In doing so, I moved it from my "Secret" window to my "Open" window. It's much harder to move things from your "Open" window to your "Secret" window. Some people resort to running away and trying to start over in order to move things from the "Open" window to the "Secret" window.**

In the bottom left section of the square, write the word "Blind." In the bottom right section, write the word "Subconscious." Explain: **The bottom panes in the window represent things that I don't know about myself. Things in the "Blind" window can be seen by others, but not by me. These might include a piece of spinach between my teeth or the fact that my laugh really irritates other people.** Have group members suggest some other examples of things that might be in a person's "Blind" window.

Then say: **If what's in my "Blind" window is important and if you care about me, you can tell me about it, helping me move it from my "Blind" window to my "Open" window. Then I can decide what to do about it.**

Things in the "Subconscious" window cannot be seen by others or by me. Have group members suggest some examples of things that might be in a person's "Subconscious" window.

Then say: **Sometimes things can move out of the "Subconscious" window. For example, some people have recalled sexual abuse from earlier in their lives. Many of these people knew what had happened, but didn't want to think about it. When they were able to start dealing with it, it emerged.**

Give group members an opportunity to ask any questions or make any comments they may have about the Johari Window. Then say: **This diagram doesn't solve anything. It's an inventory of my life. It requires honestly admitting that there are things *you* don't know about me and that there are things *I* don't even know about me.**

Allow some time for group members to fill in their Johari Windows. In the "Open" window, have kids write down some things about themselves that both they and others can see.

In the "Secret" window, have kids write down some things about themselves that they can see, but that others can't see. Emphasize that no one else will see their sheet.

In the "Blind" window, have kids write down some things about themselves that others have helped them recognize in the past—things that the kids couldn't necessarily see for themselves. For example, some kids may have discovered from others that their sarcasm was far more hurtful than they thought it was.

In the "Subconscious" window, have kids write down something about themselves that at one time was hidden from both themselves and from others. For example, a person might be so angry at his father—and so uncomfortable about his feelings—that he just doesn't think about his father at all.

After a few minutes, ask volunteers to share some things from their Johari Windows that they're comfortable talking about with the group. See how many "Secret" things—particularly those that have to do with habits and addictions—your kids are willing to share.

As you wrap up the session, give your group members an opportunity to share their thoughts regarding the things you've discussed. Use the following questions to guide your discussion.

• If one of your friends asked you what you learned in this session, what would you say?

• Have you found any answers regarding a habit or addiction you're currently facing? If so, share anything that you're comfortable talking about.

• Have you thought of any new questions? If so, what are they?

• Is there anything you want to do as a result of the stuff we've talked about in this session? If so, what?

• What would you like the rest of us to pray for you?

• What would you like to say to God about the things we've talked about in this session? Give kids an opportunity to pray silently or out loud (whichever they prefer); then close the session by praying for your group members according to the requests they listed for question 5.

The Invitation

C*O*N*T*R*O*L
A small group program for high schoolers

Everyone faces problems in his or her life. Some of the problems are minor; others are serious. CONTROL was created to help you zero in on the problems that threaten to control your life.

"Oh, I don't have any of *those* kinds of problems," you may be saying. Well, not so fast. Do you ever find yourself doing things that surprise you, things you didn't set out to do—maybe even things you swore you wouldn't do?

Eating too much, **sleeping too much**, nail biting, **DRINKING**, sexual compulsiveness, **showing off**, *intense anger*, **saying yes when you mean no**, **saying no for no good reason**, compulsive cleaning, *unreasonable fear*, insomnia, jumping trains, *people pleasing*, **burning things**, having to be right, ***driving fast***, nicotine addiction, **pimple popping**, finger drumming, GAMBLING, *bad-mouthing others*, **FIGHTING**, keeping people waiting, **lying**, compulsive exercise, *exaggerating, fantasizing*, breaking things, TURNING EVERYTHING INTO A JOKE, perfectionism, conformity

---

Is anything in this box a problem for you?

If one or more of these problems are present in your life, it's likely that there may be something else going on beneath the surface. Maybe you know immediately what that "something else" is; maybe you don't have a clue.

CONTROL will help you identify things that could become life-controlling problems. And once you've identified these problems, you'll be able to take the necessary steps to control them, instead of allowing them to control you.

If this group seems like something you want to check out, join us _____ at _____
                                                                        (date)   *(location)*
. There's no pressure. It's completely confidential and Bible-centered. If you come once and then decide it's not for you, that's fine. Questions? Call _____
                                                                (leader)

ATTRACTIONS

anger
approval
art
attractiveness
being good
being helpful
being loved
being nice
being right
being taken care of
breaking things
burning things
calendars
cars
causes
chewing things
children
cleanliness
comparisons
competence
competition
computers
conformity
contests
death
depression
dreams
drinking
driving fast
drugs
eating
envy
exaggerating

exercise
fame
family
fantasies
finger drumming
fishing
food
friends
furniture
gambling
gardening
gossiping
groups
guilt
hair twisting
happiness
housekeeping
humor
hunting
intimacy
jealousy
knowledge
lying
marriage
meeting expectations
memories
messiness
money
movies
music
nail biting
neatness
performance

pets
pimple squeezing
politics
popularity
power
psychotherapy
punctuality
reading
relationships
responsibility
revenge
scab picking
seductiveness
self-improvement
sex
shoplifting
showing off
sleeping
sports
standing out
status
stock market
stress
sunbathing
suspiciousness
talking
television
time
weight
winning
work
worthiness
writing things down

AVERSIONS

airplanes	dependence	people of different sex
anchovies	dirt	people who are addicted
anger	disapproval	people who are competent
being abnormal	doctors	people who are fat/thin
being alone	embarrassment	people who are ignorant
being discounted	evil spirits	people who are neat/messy
being fat	failure	people who are rich/poor
being judged	fire	public speaking
being overwhelmed	germs	rats
being thin	guilt	rejection
being tricked	high places	responsibility
birds	illness	sex
blood	independence	sharp instruments
boredom	intimacy	slimy creatures
bridges	mice	snakes
bugs	needles	spiders
cats	open spaces	storms
closed-in spaces	pain	strangers
commitment	people of different beliefs	success
conflict	people of different class	tests
crowds	people of different culture	traffic
darkness	people of different politics	tunnels
death	people of different race	vulnerability
dentists	people of different religion	water

Step 2

When you go through the attractions and aversions on this sheet, have kids form groups of three. Divide the items on each list among your trios so that each group has an approximately equal number. Then make your trios responsible for coming up with appropriate actions to demonstrate the things they have been assigned. In each case, the "action" should be little more than a quick pose before moving on to the next item. No item should require more than a couple of seconds. ("Cleanliness" could be shown by two people "nit-picking" every little thing off the third person; "family" could be demonstrated by striking a pose for a family photo; "fame" could be shown by two kneeling photographers taking pictures of the third; and so on.) To keep the pace going, you should read the items on the list one at a time, and move on to the next one as quickly as groups can keep up. Do the attractions first. If time permits, move on to the aversions after kids catch on.

Step 4

As you describe the Johari Window, try to devise a way to let kids act out what you're saying. After drawing a Johari Window on the board to let kids see what you're talking about, create the same thing on the floor. Explain that this is *your* Johari Window; let kids represent some of your various thoughts. Demonstrate how some thoughts (people) can move from the Secret section to the Open section, or from the Blind section to the Open section. (Put your attentive people in the Open and Subconscious sections so that they will just stand there and pay attention. Let your more active kids do the moving around so that they will continue to pay attention.)

Step 2

After kids look through the lists of attractions and aversions on Repro Resource 7, and after they work through most of the discussion questions in Step 2, ask them to make "top ten lists" of things that apply to them. They may select ten items from each list if they identify that many, or they may make their selection of ten items from both lists combined. Encourage, but don't require, kids to share one thing from their lists. (It need not be the #1 item, but rather should be something that they don't mind other people knowing about.) For one thing, this will make kids vulnerable to the group. For another, they may discover that others are secretly struggling in areas that *they* are struggling with.

Step 4

Members of a small group have the opportunity to get to know each other closely, but sometimes don't take advantage of this privilege. One nonthreatening way to do this on a regular basis is to have each person share his or her "best thing" and "worst thing" of the week at each meeting. It doesn't take long to do, but it quickly involves members in each other's lives. One person might have a crisis one week that someone else has a couple of months later, and will be able to offer comfort or advice. Kids may stop feeling so alone, even though they are few in number. They may become more willing to open up to the others. Don't expect miracles at first, but if you start this practice now and continue it on a weekly basis, you may be surprised at the positive results it will have on your group members.

Step 1

Have kids form several teams (of no less than five people) for the introductory song-naming game. But rather than having teams sing portions of songs, let them brainstorm titles instead. Explain, however, that the only songs they will get points for are those that no other teams mention. Try to keep the categories broad, to allow for the widest possibility of titles. (In addition to the categories mentioned in the session, you can add songs with a number in the title, songs about animals, songs about geographical locations, and so forth.) Allow two or three minutes for each round. Let each team list its songs as other teams cross off duplications. When all of the teams have read their lists, tally points for each answer not named by the other teams, and move on to the next category.

Step 2

Before you deal with Repro Resource 7 seriously, take a somewhat lighthearted approach to it. Have each person in your group write a "personal ad" using the list of attractions for "turn-ons" and the list of aversions as "turn-offs." Everyone should select five items from each list. After a few minutes, have everyone read his or her ad. As this is going on, other group members should see how many of their ten listed items match up with other people in the group. If any couples match more than five times, perhaps you should take a collection from group members to send them on a date.

Step 1

Kids who think they've heard it all before may be bored by a traditional review of material covered in previous sessions. So instead of using the questions in the session plan regarding how habits grow and addictions, allow kids to come up with their own review questions. Have kids form two teams. Give each team a few minutes to come up with three review questions designed to stump the other team. Emphasize that each team must be able to answer any question it comes up with. As the teams challenge each other, award one point for each question that a team answers correctly and one point for each question that stumps an opponent. You should serve as judge to make sure that the questions do indeed cover material from previous sessions and that they aren't too obscure.

Step 4

To introduce the "Blind" section of the Johari Window, have kids play a quick game. Before the session, you'll need to prepare several index cards—one for each group member. Write on each card some kind of personal statement. For example, you might use statements like "I'm mad at my mother" or "I'm afraid of being laughed at." At this point in the session, tape one card to the back of each group member without letting him or her see what's on the card. Explain that the object of the game is for group members to help each other guess what's on their cards by acting out the statements charades-style. Emphasize that no one may talk during the activity. See how long it takes for kids to guess what's on their cards based on the action clues given by other group members.

Step 3

Bring in a variety of pots, pans, and containers. One should be a cheap clay flowerpot; you should also have stainless steel, plastic, and other kinds of containers. Before you get into the Bible study, display the containers on a table. Ask: **Which of these things do you think best represents a Christian? Why?** Let kids respond, though they will probably be a bit confused at this point. Continue: **Let's see how these different specimens respond to pressure.** Toss a hefty steel pot into the air, letting it clang down on the floor unharmed. Then try a plastic container. Save the clay pot for last. Toss it into the air and let it shatter on the floor. Then have kids read II Corinthians 4:1-11. Explain that we exist only through God's power. We are much weaker than we like to think. That's why it's so important to confront any bad habits or addictions that threaten to weaken us further.

Step 4

Postpone discussing James 5:16 until Step 4. Let kids focus exclusively on the II Corinthians 4:1-11 passage first. After working through the Johari Window exercise, introduce what James has to say. Ask: **Based on this model, why do you think it is important to confess sins to each other?** If kids don't begin to make the connection on their own, show that by establishing a degree of intimacy with others, we move things from "Secret" to "Open." If we never confess sins, our "Open" lives appear much purer than they actually are. But as we become more honest with others, they might feel more free to admit their own mistakes. They might also become comfortable enough to point out things that we are "Blind" to. If we never confess faults and personal shortcomings to others, these other benefits might not occur.

Step 1

Before the session, write phrases from the old Robert Palmer song "Addicted to Love" on slips of paper. As your group members arrive, hand out the slips in random order. Explain that your kids' assignment is to arrange themselves according to the correct order of the lyrics. If kids are not familiar with the song, this could turn out to be quite interesting! When they're done, have them read (or sing) their lyrics in order. Afterward, ask: **What do you think of these lyrics?** Get a few responses. **What things, besides love, do people get addicted to?** Discuss group members' ideas. **What do you think is the difference between a habit and an addiction?**

Step 4

As you wrap up the session, read James 5:16 again. Then say: **There are many ways that God can heal us. He sometimes works through doctors to heal us physically. He sometimes works through a pastor or another strong Christian to heal us spiritually. And He sometimes works through friends or Christian counselors to heal us emotionally.** Hand out paper and pencils. Instruct group members to write a prayer to God, thanking Him for the ways in which He has healed them in the past and asking for any special healing needed now. Close the session in prayer.

Step 2

After distributing copies of Repro Resource 7, ask: **Are there things on either of these lists that you think girls would struggle with more than guys would? If so, what are they?** Make a list of group members' suggestions; then ask if there are any other things that should be added to the lists. (One item in particular that may touch the lives of your high school girls that's not on the list is shopping.) Discuss as a group what could be done to help someone struggling with particular issues on the list.

Step 3

After reading and discussing II Corinthians 4:1-11, hand out modeling clay. Instruct your girls to "sculpt" an interpretation of this passage. For instance, they might show how God has protected them when rough times have come (vss. 8, 9), what they think of the treasure in the clay jar, how Jesus' life is revealed through us, etc. Encourage kids to dig into the passage and be creative. After a few minutes, ask volunteers to share and explain their creations.

Step 2

Have your guys go through the list of attractions and aversions on Repro Resource 7. Beside each thing listed, have them place an "M" if they think it is primarily a male problem, an "F" if they think it is primarily a female problem, and a "B" if they feel both genders are affected about equally. When they finish, have one person read his list of primarily male problems as others see if they made the same observation. In many cases, your guys won't agree, which is the point of this exercise. Some of your guys are going to recognize problems that others ignore or overlook. The next volunteer may then read his list of primarily female problems, and again the rest of the group can chime in with agreement or disagreement. After generating some good discussion, move on with the session.

Step 4

After you present the Johari Window, have your group members debate whether guys are usually less "Open" about themselves than girls are. If there is some natural disagreement among your guys, let those people form opposing teams. If everyone is essentially in agreement one way or the other, then ask some of your guys who like to argue to take an opposing viewpoint. After the debate, ask: **Do you think most people could be more open than they are?** There should be little resistance to this suggestion. Explain that when people need fresh air, they open a window. Encourage your guys to "open a window" (in the interpersonal sense) every day. Most guys will need to be reminded on a regular basis, so have them decide now what they will use as a reminder (perhaps a note in their lockers or a bookmark that reads "Open a Window").

Step 1

Use the game "Song Burst" or some similar music trivia game to begin the session. More than likely, you won't have time to play the game as designed. Instead, have kids form two teams; use the game cards to begin a lyric for one team at a time. If members of the team can complete the lyric correctly, they score a point. If they can't and the other team can, the other team scores a point. After a while, when group members' minds are on music, move on to the opening activity of the session using the two teams you've already formed.

Step 4

You began the session by playing "Name That Tune." Conclude it by playing "Tune That Name." The goal should be for each person to insert his or her own name into an existing melody and write a couple of lines of lyrics about becoming more open, breaking free of addictions, improving habits, and so forth. For example, Linda might use the tune of "Twinkle, Twinkle, Little Star" to go with the following lyrics: "Linda still has far to go/But she's getting better, though/If she shares what's on her heart/That will give her a good start/Please help Linda find a way/To get better day by day."

Step 1

As an option for the opening song activity, find a copy of "Play It by Ear." There are at least two versions of the game, both of which contain a CD with short clips of popular music, movies, TV themes and quotes, tongue twisters, memory exercises, and more. If you want to confine the opening game exclusively to music, you'll need to listen to the CD ahead of time and note which of the segments contain songs. Otherwise, adapt the whole game for group competition, awarding points for either the first team to answer in each case, or for every team that answers correctly. Of course, if you use this option, you'll need to come up with your own "clips" about addiction—from songs, TV shows, movies, or wherever.

Step 4

A movie that deals with the secret side of addiction is *When a Man Loves a Woman*. It details a woman's struggle with alcoholism and the effect it has on her husband and children. If you don't have time to watch the entire video, you might want to cue up portions (which you've prescreened) dealing with the character's efforts to keep her problem secret and her resistance to getting help. While none of your group members may be to this stage in any of their own problems, the point is to let kids see what can happen so that they *never get there*.

Step 1

Try a shorter opener. Explain to your group members that you will call out a category and then name four or five items in that category. When you do, kids should form groups based on the category items. For instance, if the category was "Tastiest Ice Cream Flavor," you might list chocolate, vanilla, strawberry, cookies and cream, and mint chocolate chip. Kids would then form small groups as quickly as possible based on which of the flavors they consider to be tastiest. As soon as the groups are formed, call out another category and set of items and have kids form new groups. Continue this for several rounds. For your last category, use "Methods for Dealing with Habits." Call out just two items in the category: "In a group setting" and "By yourself." See how kids respond. Skip the review questions and Repro Resource 6. Move directly to Step 2.

Step 2

Rather than handing out Repro Resource 7, ask group members to name as many habits as they can think of that could become addictions. List group members' responses on the board. If you find that your kids are giving you predictable answers like "drinking" and "taking drugs," read some of the more unusual attractions and aversions on Repro Resource 7 and have kids respond to them. After reading the definition of *addiction*, briefly discuss whether any of your group members' past or present habits could be called addictions; then move on to Step 3.

Step 2

The first reaction of some of your kids may be to scoff at some of the attractions and aversions listed on Repro Resource 7 and to make fun of anyone who's attracted to or averse to those things. To help correct this attitude, have kids form pairs to work on a "top five list" for one of the items on Repro Resource 7. Instruct each pair to choose one of the more unusual attractions or aversions listed on the sheet and come up with five legitimate reasons why a person might be attracted to or averse to that item. After a few minutes, have each pair share its list.

Step 3

After James 5:16 is read aloud, hand out four index cards and a pencil to each group member. Instruct kids to label one card "Parent(s)," one card "Brother/Sister," one card "Best Friend," and one card "People in This Group." Then ask group members to write down on the appropriate card how they think each person (or persons) would respond if they were to confess their worst habit to him or her. After a few minutes, ask volunteers to share what they wrote down—without revealing their habits.

Step 1

Rather than using Repro Resource 6, have kids form teams. Instruct the members of each team to brainstorm a list of as many addictions as they can think of. After a few minutes, have each team share its list. Make a composite list of addictions on the board. Go through the list, briefly discussing why each thing is addictive. Then refer to the addictions listed in the box on Repro Resource 6. Write that list on the board next to the first one. Then ask: **Do any of the things on this second list surprise you? Why or why not?** Get a few responses. **What do you think people can do to get rid of an addiction?** (The first and most difficult step is to recognize the addiction. The second step will vary depending on the type and severity of the addiction, but basically it involves getting help.) **Why do you think some people refuse to do anything about their addictions, even when help is available?**

Step 4

Have group members refer to the lists of addictions you created earlier (see the "Combined Junior High/High School" option for Step 1) as well as the lists on Repro Resource 7. Distribute paper and creative materials. Instruct group members to draw (or paint or write about) something from these lists that is or could become an addiction for them. Assure them no one else will see their papers. After kids have completed their addiction identifications, challenge them to spend a few minutes in prayer, offering their problem to God and asking for His help in overcoming it.

Step 2

Try to find a copy of the book referred to in the session, *Addiction and Grace* (Gerald May, Harper San Francisco). Have some volunteers leaf through it during the first part of the meeting, looking for quotes and short segments they think might be particularly relevant to the group. Then see if someone will read and report on designated chapters at later meetings. Also provide other resources you may be familiar with for group members to examine.

Step 4

Try to help kids see the reality of what you've been discussing in these sessions. Although you're probably dealing with the material once a week or so, challenge kids to begin discussions with other people during the week to gather information about bad habits and addictions. Some of your group members' best friends who aren't in your group may be able to provide a lot of added insight—either through confrontation with these issues due to personal or family problems, or through their denial of obvious problems in their lives. Your group members should be able to learn from both positive and negative examples.

Date Used:

Approx.
Time

Step 1: Tuning Up _____
o Large Group
o Heard It All Before
o Fellowship & Worship
o Extra Fun
o Media
o Short Meeting Time
o Combined Junior High/High School
Things needed:

Step 2: Run Away, Come Closer _____
o Extra Action
o Small Group
o Large Group
o Mostly Girls
o Mostly Guys
o Short Meeting Time
o Urban
o Extra Challenge
Things needed:

Step 3: Hard Pressed _____
o Little Bible Background
o Mostly Girls
o Urban
Things needed:

Step 4: A Window View _____
o Extra Action
o Small Group
o Heard It All Before
o Little Bible Background
o Fellowship & Worship
o Mostly Guys
o Extra Fun
o Media
o Combined Junior High/High School
o Extra Challenge
Things needed:

SESSION 4

Helpless but Not Hopeless

YOUR GOALS FOR THIS SESSION:

Choose one or more

- [ ] To help kids learn the principles of self-assessment.
- [ ] To help kids understand what kinds of things hinder self-assessment.
- [ ] To help kids perform honest self-assessments.
- [ ] Other ______________________________

Your Bible Base:

Colossians 3:1-10

It Was a Dark and Stormy Night

Begin the session by reading the following situation to your group members. Explain that as you read the situation, you want kids to perform the actions. For instance, if you mention walking down the street, kids should walk in place; if you mention running, kids should run in place. You might also designate one or two group members to create other sound effects that are mentioned in the story.

Say: **You're walking down a dark street. It's late. You pull your jacket up around your neck to block the chill. You wish you weren't alone. But then you suddenly freeze as you realize that you may not be. You hear footsteps in the distance behind you. At least, you *think* they're footsteps. You listen carefully. The sound is momentarily drowned out when a car with its stereo blasting passes by on the next block. As the car noise fades, you hear the footsteps again. This time, they're closer than you thought.**

Stop the action for a moment. Ask: **What are you feeling right now? Note that I didn't ask "What would you *do*?" I asked "What are you *feeling*?"** Get several responses. Pay particular attention to the exact words kids use to describe their feelings.

Continue the activity. Say: **When you hear the footsteps a second time, you start walking again. But this time you quicken your pace. The footsteps speed up to match yours. You're two blocks from home, on a street with no streetlights, and you don't know any of your neighbors.**

Stop the action. Ask: **What are you feeling right now?** Get a few responses. Pay particular attention to the exact words kids use to describe their feelings.

Continue the activity, increasing your pace as you read. Say: **You pick up your pace even more. As you do, the footsteps behind you break into a run, closing fast on you.**

Stop the action. Ask: **What are you feeling right now?** Get a few responses. Pay particular attention to the exact words kids use to describe their feelings.

Continue the activity. Say: **The way you figure it, you've got three choices: run for your life, stand and fight, or pass out on the sidewalk. Just as you're starting to make your move to do one of the three, you hear your name being called.**

Then you feel arms grab you from behind. You'd know the voice anywhere. It's your best friend! Your closest friend in the world just rushed up behind you and gave you heart failure!

Ask: **What are you feeling right now?** Get several responses. Again, pay particular attention to the exact words kids use to describe their feelings.

Afterward, discuss the activity, using the following questions:

• **How accurate would you say your emotional response was at the beginning of the story when you consider the way the story turned out?**

• **If your emotions were not exactly accurate, would you say that they were wrong? Why or why not?**

• **How extreme was your "emotional imagination"? Did you feel nothing? Did you feel panic? How would you describe it?**

Encourage discussion and debate among your group members as they respond to these questions.

STEP 2

Vocabulary Test

(Needed: Copies of Repro Resource 8, chalkboard and chalk or newsprint and marker)

Hand out copies of "Emotional Vocabulary" (Repro Resource 8). Explain: **Many of us have a pretty limited vocabulary to describe what we feel. A lot of us have only an "on/off switch." We're either happy or sad. We're either really up or really down. But when you think about it, there's a pretty big difference between feeling frustrated and feeling angry, between feeling contented and feeling elated. If happy and sad are all we know, then we're emotionally ignorant.**

It's not because we don't have other emotions; it's just that we don't know how to describe them or how to react when we experience them. The more specifically we identify an emotion, the more control we have when we decide what to do about it.

Refer group members to the list of feeling words on Repro Resource 8. Give kids a few minutes to read through the sheet. If you have time,

OPTIONS

EXTRA ACTION

SMALL GROUP

HEARD IT ALL BEFORE

LITTLE BIBLE BACKGROUND

MOSTLY GIRLS

MOSTLY GUYS

EXTRA FUN

SHORT MEETING TIME

JR. HIGH / HIGH SCHOOL COMBINED

randomly assign one of the words on the sheet to each person. That person should then think of a specific situation in which he or she might experience that emotion. After a few minutes, have each person share the situation he or she came up with.

Point out that with a little thought, "general" emotion words can be narrowed down to identify more specific emotions. Use the following example to demonstrate what you're talking about.

Say: **Let's say I'm a teenager whose parents are divorced. I live with my mom. My dad promised to pick me up on Saturday to take me to a ball game. As usual, he didn't show up. So if you were to ask me what's wrong, I might say, "I'm** *angry* **at my dad because he didn't show up."** On the board, write "I'm ANGRY because my dad didn't show up."

Then say: **However, if I were to dig a little deeper, I might come up with a more specific emotion. For instance, I might say, "Actually, I'm** *frustrated* **because I wanted to get out of the house."** On the board, write "I'm FRUSTRATED because I wanted to get out of the house."

Then say: **And if I were to dig deeper still, I might come up with an even more specific emotion. For instance, I might say, "OK, so maybe I'm** *disappointed* **because my dad broke another promise. I don't know when to believe him anymore."** On the board, write "I'm DISAPPOINTED because my dad broke another promise."

Then say: **And if I were to dig even deeper still, I might come up with an even more specific emotion. For instance, I might say, "Really, I suppose I'm** *hurt* **because I don't know if I matter to my dad at all. And that's a pretty bad feeling."** On the board, write "I'm HURT because I don't know if I matter to my dad at all."

Note that as the identification process got more specific, the emotions changed. What started out as anger ended up as hurt. That's not to say that anger, frustration, and disappointment weren't valid emotions; the point is that the "root" emotion was hurt.

Ask one of your group members to think of a recent situation that caused him or her to be angry, happy, sad, or afraid. Then, as a group, use a process similar to the one you just used to narrow down the person's emotions. However, be careful not to put the person on the spot or to make him or her reveal emotions that he or she isn't comfortable sharing.

Afterward, ask for questions and comments regarding the process of narrowing down one's emotions.

How to Respond?

(Needed: Chalkboard and chalk or newsprint and marker)

Explain: **When we identify a feeling, it's like starting up a computer—a menu of choices presents itself to us, allowing us to decide what we want to do.**

Refer back to the "footsteps" activity you used at the beginning of the session. Ask: **For the person experiencing panic in this situation, what are some of the things he or she can choose to do?** (Keep walking, run, scream for help, fight, try to talk to the person following him or her, pretend to be crazy, fake a seizure, faint.)

Then ask: **Which of these things would you choose? Why?** Get several responses.

Say: **In the example we used earlier—the one in which my father didn't show up to take me to the ball game—we identified four possible emotions that I might have experienced: anger, frustration, disappointment, and hurt. Let's say I settled on anger. What might be on the menu of possible choices toward my dad?** Encourage several group members to offer suggestions. For example, one response might be to lash out at the undependable father. Write group members' suggestions on the board.

Then say: **What if I narrowed down my emotions to discover that I felt hurt? How might that change my menu of choices?** Ask group members to suggest several ways that a person who is hurt might respond. Emphasize that not all of the responses have to be directed at the father. Some people might respond to hurt in ways that are damaging to themselves—perhaps through some kind of compulsive behavior. Again, write group members' responses on the board.

After you've gotten several suggestions, point out: **If I choose a response that is destructive, I get one result; if I choose a response that is constructive, I get another result. If I do something creative, the situation goes one way; if I do something unimaginative, it goes another way. So the more detailed I am in identifying my feelings, the more control I have when I decide how to act on them.**

As you wrap up this section, ask: **Do you believe that you have a choice in how you react to strong emotions like fear, anger, hilarity, or arousal? Why or why not?** Encourage most of your group members to offer their opinions.

Renewal and Renovation

(Needed: Bibles, copies of Repro Resource 9)

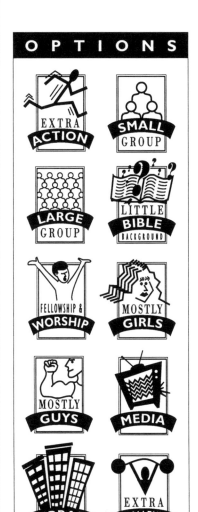

OPTIONS

Hand out copies of "Games People Play" (Repro Resource 9). Explain that the items listed on the sheet are things that can block self-assessment and self-control. Go through the sheet as a group, first discussing how the items on the sheet might hinder a person who is trying to assess his or her emotions, and then discussing how the items might hinder a person who is trying to assess a personal habit.

Say: **Admitting that a habit has taken control of your life is very difficult to do. People in the Alcoholics Anonymous program admit that they are powerless over alcohol and that their lives have become unmanageable as a result. Many others can substitute the word "alcohol" with any of several other things that have made their lives unmanageable.**

So if a person is powerless against a certain habit, and if his or her life is unmanageable as a result, what can he or she do? (The only choice that makes sense is for the person to humbly admit that he or she needs *God's* power.)

Ask: **What do you think of the "games people play"? Have you ever played any of these games to avoid surrendering your own habits to God? If so, explain.** Encourage several group members to respond. Emphasize that they need not reveal their habits to the group.

Have someone read aloud Colossians 3:1-10. Then ask: **What stands out to you in this passage? Why?** Get a few responses.

Ask: **What do you think it means to set your heart and mind on things above?** (Perhaps it means concentrating on things that will please God.)

When have you been most successful at setting your heart and mind on things above? Why do you suppose that is?

When have you been least successful at setting your heart and mind on things above? Why do you suppose that is?

What do you think it means to put to death whatever belongs to your earthly nature? (Perhaps it means actively trying to rid your life of things that are displeasing to God.) **How successful have you been at doing that? Explain.**

Colossians 3:9 instructs us not to lie to each other. How do you think that applies to what we're doing in this group? You might also want to look at James 5:16.

In Colossians 3:10, the word *renewed* means "renovated." Have you ever been involved in the renovation of a building or the remodeling of a room? If so, what's it like?

If God's renovation of your life is like remodeling a building, what does that tell you about the cost in time and in the deconstruction that may have to take place before the re-construction is completed?

As you wrap up the session, give your group members an opportunity to share their thoughts regarding the things you've discussed. Use the following questions to guide your discussion.

• **If one of your friends asked you what you learned in this session, what would you say?**

• **Is there anything you want to do as a result of the stuff we've talked about in this session? If so, what?**

• **Have you discovered anything new about yourself or about the group? If so, what?**

• **What would you like the rest of us to pray for you?**

• **What would you like to say to God about the things we've talked about in this session?** Give kids an opportunity to pray silently or out loud (whichever they prefer); then close the session by praying for your group members according to the requests they listed for question 4.

HAPPY
accepted
appreciated
blissful
calm
capable
carefree
cheerful
comfortable
confident
content
delighted
ecstatic
elated
encouraged
enthusiastic
exhilarated
giddy
glad
gleeful
grateful
hopeful
inspired
jolly
joyous
lighthearted
lively
loved
merry
needed
optimistic
overjoyed
peaceful
playful
pleased
satisfied
secure
serene
spirited
sunny
thankful
tranquil
warm

UNHAPPY
bored
bothered
cheerless
choked up
cloudy
dejected
depressed
despondent
disappointed
discontented
discouraged
disheartened
distracted
downcast

dreary
gloomy
glum
joyless
melancholy
moody
mournful
oppressed
quiet
sad
somber
sorrowful
sulky
sullen
upset
woeful

ANGRY
annoyed
belligerent
bitter
bugged
contemptuous
defiant
disgusted
enraged
exasperated
fuming
incensed
indignant
infuriated
irate
irritated
mad
peeved
perturbed
riled
seething
ticked off
worked up
wrathful

HURT
abandoned
accused
aching
afflicted
agonized
belittled
betrayed
defensive
degraded
deprived
disrespected
grieved
injured
left out
let down
misused

offended
pathetic
persecuted
provoked
put down
resentful
taken advantage of
tortured
unappreciated
unimportant
unloved
untrusted
used
victimized
woeful
worried

OVERWHELMED
astounded
beaten
bewildered
blown away
broken
cold
crushed
deflated
demotivated
dull
dumbfounded
empty
exhausted
flat
floored
grief-stricken
heartbroken
helpless
hollow
humble
humiliated
in despair
inconsolable
insecure
like giving up
lost
low
miserable
mortified
nauseated
numb
panicky
paralyzed
pessimistic
plagued
powerless
shaken
sick
staggered
stumped
stunned

tired
weary
worn out

EXCITED
bold
brave
calm
certain
confident
determined
fearless
firm
hungry
impatient
resolved
self-reliant
strong

ANXIOUS
absorbed
agitated
alone
apprehensive
cautious
concerned
curious
dependent
distant
distressed
distrustful
doubtful
eager
engrossed
fascinated
hesitant
indecisive
inquisitive
intent
interested
intrigued
itchy
nosy
perplexed
questioning
skeptical
snoopy
suspicious
unbelieving
uncertain
uneasy
uptight
wavering

AFRAID
aghast
alarmed
appalled
apprehensive

awed
chicken
cowardly
dismayed
fainthearted
fearful
fidgety
frightened
hesitant
horrified
hysterical
immobilized
insecure
lonely
nervous
panicky
petrified
restless
scared
shaky
sheepish
suspicious
terrified
threatened
timid
trembly

GUILTY
ashamed
bad
dumb
embarrassed
foolish
incompetent
infantile
like a failure
naive
remorseful
repentant
ridiculous
self-conscious
selfish
silly
slow
stupid
unfit
useless
weird
worthless
wrong

SYMPATHETIC
compassionate
concerned
connected
empathetic
moved
understanding

GAMES PEOPLE PLAY

JUSTIFICATION
"I do it because _____.
If you were in my shoes, you'd do it too."

RATIONALIZATION
"I can't do anything about it, because . . ."

BLAMING
"It's his fault. He makes me so mad that I . . ."

PLAYING DUMB
"I don't know why I do it."

DENIAL
"I don't do that."

MINIMIZING
"Lighten up. It's not a big deal."

WITHDRAWAL
"I'd prefer not to talk about it."

SMUGNESS
"This is me—I can handle it."

HUMOR
"So I'm a little messed up. Tell me something I don't know."

APATHY
"Tell someone who cares."

DELAY
"You're right. I'm going to do something about it soon."

DEFLECTION
"That reminds me—did you see the movie about that guy who . . ."

ANGER
"Leave me alone!"

SARCASM
"Why don't you get a life so you can get out of mine?"

AVOIDANCE
"If I can just stay busy, I won't think about it."

COMPARING
"At least I'm not as bad as . . ."

EXTRA ACTION

Step 2
Have kids form teams to play a version of Pictionary. Give each team one set of words listed on Repro Resource 8, cut apart on individual slips of paper. At your signal, the first person on each team will choose one of the slips, look at the word, and begin to draw it for other team members. When he or she is finished, the next person will draw a slip and continue the process. See how many words each team can guess correctly in five minutes. Score one point for every word guessed. Explain that everyone must take part equally in the drawing responsibilities. If team members cannot guess the word being drawn, the person may pass and let the next person take over. But every pass will cost the team one point. Award prizes to the winning team, if you wish.

Step 4
Have kids form teams for a relay. Line the teams up at one end of the room. At the other end of the room, place a number of blocks, dominoes, or some other building materials stacked in a particular way. You need one identical stack for each team. Everyone needs to know exactly how the blocks are stacked. The first person on each team must knock the stack flat—with no two blocks remaining on top of each other. The next person in line must reconstruct the stack to its original shape. Keep alternating for a period of time, after which you give a signal to stop. The team that has rotated the most members is the winner. Use this activity in connection with your closing words on the meaning of *renewed* (Colossians 3:10). Explain that just as the blocks were "renovated" several times during the relay, God has the power to renew us whenever we feel "flattened" by the events of life or by our own hard-to-break habits.

SMALL GROUP

Step 2
Come up with several situations that will trigger certain feelings. When you ask kids to tell you what feeling they would expect in each situation, no two people should give the same answer, though everyone should answer truthfully. For example, you might say: **Your parents forgot your birthday yesterday and didn't remember until today. How do you feel?** If the first person responds "Hurt," no one else may use that answer. After the first situation, explain that you won't accept answers that have been used for *previous* questions either. Each situation must result in an entirely unused set of responses. Afterward, hand out Repro Resource 8 to let kids see how many emotions they *didn't* think of. Here are some situations to use:
• **While grounded, you try to sneak out to see a friend—and wreck the car.**
• **You overhear a close friend spreading gossip about you.**
• **You find a $20 bill left behind by the last owner of your math book.**

Step 4
As you discuss Repro Resource 9, position kids so that they can't see each other. Read through the sixteen different items on the sheet, explaining what each one means. After you read each one, ask: **During the past week, can you think of a time when you dealt with a problem or confrontation by using this method?** Kids who have done so should raise their hands. When you finish, have everyone face one another again. Tally up the number of different ways your kids responded to difficult situations. Announce the number, determine an approximate percentage, and estimate the number of areas in which more than one person responded. Show that the tendency to avoid facing problems is widespread, so you need to commit to one another even closer in the future to do a better job of dealing with conflicts.

LARGE GROUP

Step 1
Rather than having kids act out the opening story as you read it, hand out paper and pencils and have them listen closely instead. Explain that whenever you stop the story, kids should write down exactly what they are *feeling*. There are four pauses in the story as written, but you can insert some additional ones if you wish. For example, you might want to get a response as soon as kids realize that there *might* be someone behind them. What you should try to do is provide the opportunity for kids to use a large variety of words. Afterward, as they share their responses, let them see how frequently they used the same words: *scared*, *frightened*, and so forth. Later, when you hand out Repro Resource 8, point out the breadth of vocabulary we have to work with, and challenge kids to start being more specific about their feelings.

Step 4
Have kids form teams of two or three. Assign one of the areas on Repro Resource 9 to each team. Ask group members to name some examples of serious problem situations that are common to many teenagers. Such situations might include a parent discovering that a teenage child is using drugs (or having sex), a boss getting onto a teen employee for goofing off too much on the job, or a teacher having a student stay after class to discuss his or her poor grades. For each of the situations you come up with, you should play the role of the authority figure as team members decide how a kid would respond, using whatever area (from Repro Resource 9) they were assigned. Don't let this drag out too long. Quickly move from team to team, using the same opening line and letting teams demonstrate the many different ways that kids can respond.

Step 1

Before you hand out copies of Repro Resource 8 in Step 2, give your heard-it-all-before group members an opportunity to show off their own emotional vocabularies. Have kids sit in a circle. Read a brief scenario to your group members; then have them name emotions that the person in the scenario might be experiencing. For example, you might say: **Rodney has had a crush on Julia for as long as he can remember. Today, Julia's best friend told Rodney that Julia would love to go out with him. How do you think Rodney feels?** Group members might then name emotions like "happy," "excited," "overjoyed," "relieved," and "eager." Each person will have ten seconds to come up with an emotion. If a person can't name an emotion in ten seconds, or if he or she names an emotion that's already been used, he or she is out. Continue (using different scenarios) until only one person remains. Then move on to Step 2.

Step 2

Rather than working as a group to narrow down the emotions of one person, give your kids an opportunity to work together in teams to come up with several different examples of identifying specific emotions. Have kids form four teams. Assign each team one of the major headings on Repro Resource 8—happy, unhappy, angry, hurt, etc. Instruct each team to come up with a scenario in which a person initially experiences the team's assigned emotion, but then gradually narrows down his or her feelings to discover other emotions. After a few minutes, have each team share what it came up with.

Step 2

As kids peruse the words in the emotional vocabulary, ask: **How many of these words do you think applied to Jesus at some time in His life?** Have kids circle all of the words they think apply. When they finish, let them read what they circled and explain when they think Jesus felt that way. You should have a list of your own. Kids who don't know a lot about the Bible may be surprised at the range of emotions Jesus experienced. Use this opportunity to encourage kids to read through the Gospels to see for themselves the variety of feelings Jesus had. In doing so, they may develop more patience and perseverance during their own emotional mood swings.

Step 4

Focus on Colossians 3:1, 2. Explain that the heart is the center of feelings and the mind is the center of thoughts. Ask: **Have you ever considered that you can "set your hearts" and "set your minds"? Or do you tend to be at the mercy of your thoughts and feelings?** It may be odd to some of your kids to consider that they can choose what they will think and feel. And while it is certainly not a good idea to repress strong thoughts or feelings, it is part of being "raised with Christ" (vs. 1) to learn to determine who we will follow and what we will believe. Share an example of a time when you felt an initial negative feeling, and perhaps had strong negative thoughts as well, but eventually chose not to allow those thoughts and feelings to determine your actions. Then ask kids to try to identify similar recent opportunities they have had, whether or not they chose to do anything about them. The first step they need to take is to recognize *opportunities* to decide to focus on "things above."

Step 1

To begin the session, say: **We've been discussing some pretty heavy topics. When we start seeing these habits in our lives, what are some things that can happen?** Get a few responses. If no one mentions it, suggest that when we become honest with ourselves and start seeing the negative things in our lives, Satan likes to jump in and feed on that negative stuff—causing us to get down on ourselves, have doubts, and even question whether God could love someone as bad as us. Read Romans 8:38, 39 to reassure your kids that nothing can separate us from God's love. Ask: **How does it make you feel to know that? Can you believe it?** Allow time for discussion; then thank God for His never-ending and totally unconditional love.

Step 4

Hand out paper, pencils, rulers, and markers or crayons. Picking up on the building-remodeling analogy, ask your group members to draw a house that represents their life. The condition of the house should indicate where they think they are in God's remodeling process. For instance, if they're in a "leaky faucet" stage, they should draw that. If they think God's adding a second story, they should draw that. After a few minutes, ask volunteers to display and explain their house drawings.

Step 2

Before the session, choose various emotions from those listed on Repro Resource 8; write each on a small slip of paper. Be sure to include a mixture of the more "basic" emotions (like "happy" and "sad") with some of the lesser-recognized emotions (like "warm," "slow," and "left out"). After you've looked over Repro Resource 8, say: **We're now going to play a game called "What's My Emotion?"** Explain that one person will draw a slip of paper with an emotion written on it. She must then try to get others to guess her emotion. She may use pantomime, facial expressions, and all kinds of body language, but she may not make any noise. The first person to guess correctly will then choose the next slip. After you've played a few rounds, ask: **Were some of the emotions easier to identify than others? If so, why?**

Step 4

Hand out paper and pencils. Instruct your girls to complete the following statements:
• The feeling that is easiest for me to identify is _____ because . . .
• The feeling that is hardest for me to identify is _____ because . . .
• One person I can really share my feelings with is _____ because . . .
Close the session in prayer, thanking God for giving us emotions, asking for His help in identifying emotions that we can't identify on our own, and thanking Him for the people in our lives with whom we can share our emotions.

Step 2

After you discuss the ways that people couch their true feelings (going from anger to frustration, to disappointment, to hurt), discuss this tendency specifically from a male perspective. Ask: **Why don't guys express what they are truly feeling?** Write down all of the responses you receive. Certainly there are times when guys don't actually realize their true feelings. But other times they have various reasons for wanting to disguise the truth. See how many of these reasons group members come up with. If you don't get at least a dozen good reasons right away, your guys probably aren't trying hard enough.

Step 4

Add an athletic element to the discussion of Repro Resource 9. Bring in a dart board and at least one dart. Cut apart one copy of Repro Resource 9 and staple one of the items listed on the sheet to each section of the dart board. You should have four sections left over. Keep them blank for guys to aim for and possibly miss a turn by hitting one of them. Have each group member write out three different situations that he would find annoying or aggravating. Collect those situations. Then have one guy at a time throw the dart at the dart board. If he hits one of the blank sections, he doesn't have to do anything (except look smug). If he hits one of the labeled sections, you should read one of the situations and have the guy deal with it using the method he has "selected." If the situation involves other people, you should represent them.

Step 1

This is a fairly serious session, so begin with a version of the old game show "Make Me Laugh." Select a volunteer to be the contestant. Then give three other people thirty seconds each to try to make the person laugh. This can be done by telling jokes, making faces, speaking in funny voices, or whatever. If the first person fails to make the contestant laugh, move to the second one, and then the third. If none of the three makes the person laugh, congratulate him or her and then recruit another contestant and three more comedians. Use this activity to introduce the idea that some people are much better than others at hiding what they are truly feeling.

Step 2

After you distribute copies of Repro Resource 8, play a game. Start by showing one of your group members one of the words on the sheet. That person should do anything he or she can—nonverbally—to portray that specific emotion. Other group members should guess which one it is. (They may use their sheets to do so.) After everyone guesses, the volunteer should reveal the word. Anyone who guessed correctly scores a point. Give everyone an equal number of opportunities to portray one of the emotions; that way, everyone will have an equal number of guesses and you can compare scores accurately. The scores, by the way, may be lower than most people might have expected. This exercise can be a lot of fun, but it will also clarify what a wide variety of emotions we have to deal with.

Step I

Since the goals of the session have to do with self-assessment, you might want to begin the session by having group members take an actual self-assessment test. You can make this as serious or as lighthearted as you wish. If you want a legitimate, scientific measure of personality assessment, stop by the library and find a test that you can administer yourself. (In many cases, only professionals are permitted to oversee and evaluate the process.) Or you might want to lighten up the discussion a bit and find a teen magazine with a quiz on "Ten Ways to Know Yourself Better." The goal should be to get your kids discussing their emotions and interacting with each other. During the session, have another leader or a student volunteer determine the results of each person's test. Kids aren't likely to come to any significant conclusions in a single meeting just from doing a self-assessment exercise; but if you convince them to become more open with each other, your help may be more significant than you'll ever realize.

Step 4

Many of the themes in this session are dealt with on a regular basis on "The John Larroquette Show"—especially the programs during the show's first season. The main character is a recovering alcoholic who regularly attends Alcoholics Anonymous meetings. He tries to deal openly with his emotions and his past. He is trying to get beyond denial and the other "games people play" (see Repro Resource 9). While these segments are only small portions of the program, you may want to screen a few episodes to see if you can find something that applies specifically to what you plan to cover in the session.

Step I

Rather than going through the entire story in Step I, simply read a couple of brief scenarios and ask group members to describe how they would feel in each one. Make note of your group members' emotional vocabulary as they describe how they would feel. Here are some scenarios you might use:

• **You just found out that your best friend was arrested for drunk driving.**
• **You're home alone late at night when you hear someone trying to get in your back door.**
• **You just hit the winning shot to give your team the state basketball championship.**

Use this activity to lead in to the discussion of Repro Resource 8 in Step 2.

Step 2

Rather than going through Repro Resource 8 during the session, hand it out at the end of the meeting as a take-home resource. If you used the "Short Meeting Time" option for Step I, spend some time now discussing your group members' responses. For instance, let's say that one of your group members said she would be "upset" upon hearing that her best friend was arrested for drunk driving. Ask: **What if [the name of the group member] had said that she was *gloomy*? How is that different from *upset*? What about *somber*? How is that different?** The point you're trying to make is that there are many different emotions—and the more precise we can be in identifying them, the more control we have in deciding how to act on them.

Step I

Begin the session with an activity designed to introduce the topic of self-assessment. Ask for two volunteers to receive make-overs. If possible, bring in a professional hair stylist and a makeup expert to do the make-overs. One of the volunteers should be given a make-over that makes him or her look good; the second should be given a make-over that makes him or her look bad. However, don't let your volunteers know what kind of make-overs they're receiving. (Instruct the rest of your group members to keep their comments and snickering to themselves during the make-overs.) After the make-overs, but before you give your volunteers mirrors for them to see what they look like, ask them to do self-assessments. Ask: **How do you think you look right now? What makes you think that?** After volunteers respond, give them mirrors to see how accurate their self-assessments were. Then, while the rest of the group does the opening activity in the session plan, allow your second volunteer to receive a "real" make-over.

Step 4

As you're handing out Repro Resource 9, ask each group member to think of someone he or she knows (or knows *of*) who has some kind of an addiction. Perhaps some of your kids have a friend or family member who's a drug addict. Perhaps other kids know of a homeless person in their neighborhood who's an alcoholic. Ask: **How might the person you're thinking of use one or more of the things listed on this sheet to respond to someone who confronted him or her about his or her addiction?** If possible, try to cover all sixteen items on the sheet.

Step 2
Your junior highers may find it quite challenging to narrow down their feelings as suggested in the latter part of Step 2. Many may not even realize that some of the things listed on Repro Resource 8 are feelings. Spend some extra time going through the "emotional vocabulary." Ask kids to pick out the words or phrases that they think they'd have the most difficulty identifying. Make a list of those emotions; then ask for volunteers (you may need your high schoolers to step up here) to act out scenes in which someone would have cause to feel each of the particular emotions. Allow time for discussion afterward.

Step 3
Ask: **Do you think that we can get into habits with our feelings? Explain.** Some of your group members may be stumped by this question. Ask if they've ever known someone who's always grumpy, always happy, always expressing the same emotion regardless of the situation. Point out that some people seem to have lost the ability to recognize other feelings and have learned to rely on only one or two. Ask: **Why do you think it's important to be able to identify our various feelings?** (So that we can better choose how to respond to particular situations and how to deal with our feelings.)

Step 1
After opening with the story in the session, give kids an opportunity to create stories of their own. Have them work in teams to try to write a story with pauses in appropriate places to allow other group members to identify specific feelings. Explain that the stories don't need to be scary just because the first one was. Some might be romantic, exciting, or depressing. After a few minutes, let each team read its story while everyone else responds appropriately. In each case, challenge kids to be as specific and diverse as possible in describing what they would be feeling.

Step 4
The material you've been discussing in this session (and this series) is rather weighty. If the truth of these sessions begins to soak in, it is likely to touch kids at many different levels—not just intellectually, but physically, emotionally, and spiritually as well. Group members are likely to begin asking hard questions. Perhaps they will begin to experience emotions that are new to them and will want help. If such situations arise, it may be that you don't feel qualified to handle them. At some point, you might want to bring in some professional help in the form of a Christian psychiatrist or a pastor trained in counseling. If you have your guest sit in throughout the session, perhaps he or she can pick up on significant questions or potential warning signs from some of your group members. Then, at the end of the session, you can have him or her respond to some of the things you've been discussing and answer any questions your group members have. (And if any of your kids are having more serious problems than they can discuss in a group setting, this person would be an excellent one to contact later on for help.)

Date Used:

Approx.
Time

**Step 1: It Was a Dark and
Stormy Night** _____
o Large Group
o Heard It All Before
o Fellowship & Worship
o Extra Fun
o Media
o Short Meeting Time
o Urban
o Extra Challenge
Things needed:

Step 2: Vocabulary Test _____
o Extra Action
o Small Group
o Heard It All Before
o Little Bible Background
o Mostly Girls
o Mostly Guys
o Extra Fun
o Short Meeting Time
o Combined Junior High/High School
Things needed:

Step 3: How to Respond? _____
o Combined Junior High/High School
Things needed:

**Step 4: Renewal and
Renovation** _____
o Extra Action
o Small Group
o Large Group
o Little Bible Background
o Fellowship & Worship
o Mostly Girls
o Mostly Guys
o Media
o Urban
o Extra Challenge
Things needed:

SESSION 5
Turning Stones into Bread

YOUR GOALS FOR THIS SESSION:
Choose one or more

☐ To help kids discover how God can turn weakness into strength.

☐ To help kids understand what mood management is and what it involves.

☐ To help kids learn a practical mood management technique.

☐ Other _____
_____

Your Bible Base:

II Corinthians 12:1-10
Philippians 4:8

Common Interests

OPTIONS

SMALL GROUP

LARGE GROUP

FELLOWSHIP & WORSHIP

MEDIA

SHORT MEETING TIME

URBAN

To begin the session, have kids form small groups based on common interests. For instance, one group might be made up of kids who enjoy playing sports. Another group might be made up of kids who enjoy computers. Another group might be made up of kids who enjoy service projects. Of course, your kids are likely to have more than one interest. But they shouldn't spend a lot of time trying to decide which group best suits them. Instead, they should just find a group as quickly as possible.

Once kids have assembled into groups, give them a few minutes to respond to the following questions regarding the interest they chose.

- **How did you find out that you enjoy this activity?**
- **What do you like best about it? Why?**
- **What does it feel like when things are really working well for you in this activity?** (For example, baseball players who are in the midst of a hitting streak say that they can see pitches so well at the plate that the ball looks like it's the size of a grapefruit.)
- **What does it feel like when things are really going badly for you in this activity?** (For example, baseball players who are in the midst of a hitting slump say that the ball looks like it's the size of a marble when a pitcher throws it.)

After the members of each group have had a few minutes to discuss the questions among themselves, have volunteers share some of their responses with the entire group.

Afterward, explain that you will be referring to this activity later in the session.

STEP
2

A Thorny Issue

(Needed: Bibles)

Have someone read aloud II Corinthians 12:1-10. Then ask: **What's your first impression of this passage? Explain.** Encourage several group members to respond.

Is there anything in this passage that surprises or confuses you? If so, what is it? Why is it surprising or confusing to you? You may need to explain that it's likely that the person Paul is referring to in verses 2-5 is himself. Group members may also be confused about the concept of boasting about weaknesses rather than accomplishments.

Do you identify with Paul at all in this passage? If so, in what areas? (Some group members may relate to having a "thorn" in the flesh—something that is a hindrance to them.)

Some people believe that the thorn in Paul's flesh was a physical disability. Others think that it just as likely might have been a life-controlling habit. What do you think? Why?

Point out that whether or not Paul's thorn in the flesh was a life-controlling habit, the Lord's words in verse 9—"My grace is sufficient for you, for my power is made perfect in weakness"—certainly apply to people today who are afflicted by life-controlling habits.

STEP
3

Mood Management

(Needed: Copies of Repro Resource 10, copies of Repro Resource 11, pencils)

Hand out copies of "Mood Management" (Repro Resource 10) and pencils. Explain that there are four different kinds of moods: high positive, low positive, high negative, and low negative. Emphasize that it's important to recognize our moods because bad habits and addictive

OPTIONS

EXTRA ACTION

LITTLE BIBLE BACKGROUND

MOSTLY GIRLS

MOSTLY GUYS

EXTRA FUN

behaviors are powered by negative moods.

Use the group-discussion activity in Step 1 to give group members an idea of things that can affect moods. Ask: **When things are going really well for you in the activity you chose earlier, how might that affect your mood?** (It probably would cause a person to be in a high positive mood.)

When things are going really badly in that area, how might that affect your mood? (The frustration involved probably would cause a person to be in a high negative mood.)

Give group members a few minutes to answer the questions on Repro Resource 10. When everyone is finished, ask several volunteers to share their responses to each question. Pay particular attention to how the various moods affect the way kids feel about life.

Then ask: **Which of these moods is most common for you? What percentage of your time would you say you spend in that mood?**

Which of these moods is least common for you? What percentage of your time would you say you spend in that mood? Get responses from several group members.

How do you think bad habits and addictive behaviors are powered by negative moods? Encourage most of your group members to offer their opinions. If no one mentions it, suggest that people in negative moods may be looking for things to make them feel better when they engage in bad habits and addictive behaviors.

Then ask: **Do you think moods just happen or can they be controlled? Explain.**

After you've gotten responses from several group members, hand out copies of "Mood Factors" (Repro Resource 11). Give kids a few minutes to complete the sheet. When everyone is finished, ask volunteers to describe how each of the factors on the sheet affects their moods. Then, as a group, determine which factors are most powerful in affecting moods.

Afterward, ask: **What can we learn from this sheet regarding mood management?** (Once we've determined that a certain factor affects our moods in certain ways, we can limit or regulate the input of that factor in our lives, thereby managing our moods a little more closely.)

Have someone read aloud Philippians 4:8. Then ask: **How does this verse affect your understanding of mood management? Explain.** (Concentrating on things that are true, noble, right, pure, lovely, admirable, excellent, and praiseworthy is a powerful way to combat negative moods.)

STEP

4

The HALT Method

(Needed: Paper, pencils, chalkboard and chalk or newsprint and marker)

Demonstrate for your group members a simple, practical technique for doing self-assessment and mood management throughout the day. This technique is called the "HALT" method.

Say: **When you recognize that you're in a high negative or low negative mood, pause for a moment to ask yourself four questions.** Write the following questions on the board as you name them.

- **Am I too *hungry*?**
- **Am I too *angry*?**
- **Am I too *lonely*?**
- **Am I too *tired*?**

After you've listed the questions, ask: **What happens to your mood when you get too hungry? Why?**

What happens to your mood when you get too angry? Why?

What happens to your mood when you get too lonely? Why?

What happens to your mood when you get too tired? Why? Get several responses.

Then ask: **If you recognize that you're getting hungry, angry, lonely, or tired, how might that help you combat negative moods?** (By taking such relatively simple steps as finding something to eat, giving yourself a "cool down" period, calling a friend, or going to bed early, you're removing some of the fuel that fires negative moods.)

If no one mentions it, point out that when a person combats his or her negative moods, he or she is also removing some of the "power sources" that energize bad habits and addictive behavior.

As you wrap up the session, give your group members an opportunity to share their thoughts regarding the things you've discussed. Use the following questions to guide your discussion.

- **If one of your friends asked you what you learned in this session, what would you say?**
- **Is there anything you want to do as a result of the stuff we've talked about in this session? If so, what?**
- **Have you discovered anything new about yourself or about the group? If so, what?**

• **What would you like the rest of us to pray for you?**

• **What would you like to say to God about the things we've talked about in this session?** Give kids an opportunity to pray silently or out loud (whichever they prefer); then close the session by praying for your group members according to the requests they listed for question 4.

To end this session (and this series), read aloud II Corinthians 12:9 again: "My grace is sufficient for you, for my power is made perfect in weakness." Encourage your group members to seek God's power as they continue to combat their bad habits and addictive behavior.

MOOD MANAGEMENT

HIGH POSITIVE

Up; creative; intense; focused; generous; physically, mentally, socially, and spiritually alert

1. When have you been High Positive? (For example: when performing at your peak in sports, drama, or music; in a particularly romantic setting)

2. How do you feel about life when you are High Positive?

3. What does being High Positive do to your relationships? Explain.

LOW POSITIVE

Relaxed, steady, attentive, mellow, taking things in, benevolent

1. When have you been Low Positive? (For example: late at night with friends, while telling or listening to stories; relaxing after a good meal)

2. How do you feel about life when you are Low Positive?

3. What does being Low Positive do to your relationships? Explain.

HIGH NEGATIVE

Edgy, irritated, sarcastic, angry, lashing out, vengeful, hurtful, stressed, destructive

1. When have you been High Negative? (For example: when you were in an argument; when someone cut you off in traffic)

2. How do you feel about life when you are High Negative?

3. What does being High Negative do to your relationships? Explain.

LOW NEGATIVE

Sullen, depressed, self-absorbed, unmotivated, burned out

1. When have you been Low Negative? (For example: when you were tired; when you were disappointed by someone or something)

2. How do you feel about life when you are Low Negative?

3. What does being Low Negative do to your relationships? Explain.

MOOD
FACTORS

Consider the following factors. How, if at all, might each of them contribute to your mood? Be as specific and as detailed as possible.

DIET
• *For example, when I use too much caffeine, I tend to be High Negative for a while and then Low Negative.*

REST

EXERCISE

SOCIAL CIRCUMSTANCES

STIMULANTS

DEPRESSANTS

VIDEO/TV/MOVIES

BOOKS

MUSIC

MAGAZINES

FUELERS (stronger people who encourage and help you)

DRAINERS (weaker people for whom you feel responsible)

SPIRITUAL LIFE

Step 2

Before the session, draw a large rosebush on a piece of poster board, with the leaves and blooms filled in. Also design a number of "thorns" that will fit into the picture. But rather than draw them in, make *paper* thorns that can be attached later. During the session, after you discuss Paul's thorn and whether it might be a physical ailment or a life-controlling habit, have your kids think of any such things that they are facing. Their "thorns" may be problems that are physical, emotional, spiritual, financial, or whatever. They should think of as many as they can. For everything they think of, have them write it down on one of the paper thorns. If kids don't mind sharing the "thorn" with the rest of the group, they can attach it to the rosebush face out. If they aren't ready to share it, they can fold the thorn in half, glue or staple it together, and place it on the rosebush without allowing others to see what it is. Beneath the rosebush, have someone write out the text of II Corinthians 12:7b-9. As you go through the rest of the session, make frequent reference to the "rosebush" and the "thorns" that are attached.

Step 3

As you begin this step, have kids form groups. Ask the members of each group to put together a skit of a situation that "puts them in a mood." (Be intentionally ambiguous as to what mood you want them to create. Anything goes.) After a few minutes, have the groups perform their skits. Use the skits for examples as you discuss high positive, low positive, high negative, and low negative moods. Using the skits as a starting point, you can be more specific about how to move from one area to another without becoming too personal or too threatening to anyone.

Step 1

Rather than having kids form small groups based on common interests, see how many "common threads" you can find among your group members—things that they *all* enjoy doing. If even one person doesn't truly enjoy an activity, don't include it. Whenever you find a common bond, have kids answer the questions presented in the session. Try to maintain a fairly strong pace during this time—don't let it drag. It is hoped that kids will quickly begin to see how much they have in common (after a little thought), but as soon as they begin to slow down considerably between answers, move on with the rest of the session.

Step 4

After dealing with the information in the session on an individual level, conclude the session by dealing with the information on a group level. Explain that you want to put a "HALT" to the problems in the group. Ask: **Is anyone here too hungry?** Have some special refreshments prepared for group members. As kids are eating, ask: **Is anyone here too angry?** If someone is, the rest of the group members should give that person their phone numbers and permission to call anytime during the rest of the week to "blow off steam." Then ask: **Is anyone here too lonely?** Whether anyone responds or not, instruct group members to provide hugs for each other all around. Finally, ask: **Is anyone here too tired?** As soon as kids say yes, send them home to get some rest.

Step 1

You may need a little more organization in breaking down a large group into smaller, cohesive units. Begin by determining basic categories of interests: Sports, Music, Food, Dating, and Other. Have group members choose one of those groups. Appoint a leader in each group to help it keep dividing. For instance, Sports might divide into Basketball, Football, Baseball, Soccer, and Other. Music might divide into School Band, Garage Bands, Listening to CDs, and Other. For any groups that remain too large, keep appointing leaders to further subdivide it. By the time you get down to groups of three or four, you may have some very creative distinctions to unite the small group members.

Step 4

The topic of this session (and this series) may not have appealed to everyone in your group. But in any large group there are likely to be some people ready and willing to begin to open up about their bad habits and addictions. Before you leave this topic and move on to something else, you might want to take a poll to see if anyone wishes to keep discussing the things you've addressed in this series. If so, you might consider starting a small support group (or groups) to provide helpful outlets for such people who want or need to do something about their habits and addictions. If you cannot oversee this group yourself, you should try to get a tentative commitment from someone else willing to do so before mentioning the possibility to your group members.

HEARD IT ALL BEFORE

Step 2

Kids who have grown up in the church hearing about the incredible faith and perseverance of the apostle Paul may be surprised at the "humanness" displayed by Paul in II Corinthians 12:7-10. Ask: **Why do you suppose Paul asked God three times to remove his "thorn"? Why do you think he didn't get the message the first time God refused to take it away?** Encourage several group members to offer their opinions. If you have time, it might be interesting for your group members to spend a few minutes offering conjectures as to what Paul's thorn might have been. Afterward, point out that it doesn't really matter what the thorn was; what matters is the message of II Corinthians 12:9—God's grace is sufficient for us; His power is made perfect in weakness.

Step 4

As you wrap up the session, introduce an allegorical passage written by C. S. Lewis to summarize the topic of habits. In *The Great Divorce* (New York, Collier Books, © 1946, pp. 98-103 [in the paperback edition]), Lewis imagines an encounter between an angel and a man obsessed by lust. Begin the story with the passage that reads "I saw coming towards us a Ghost who carried something on his shoulder. . . ." Conclude with the passage that reads " . . . they vanished, bright themselves, into the rose-brightness of that everlasting morning." Afterward, ask: **What do you think happened to the Lizard? How might this passage apply to your own bad habits and addictive behaviors?** Have kids silently consider the following questions: **What "lizard" in your life would you like God to transform into a "steed"? What do you think that will cost you?**

LITTLE BIBLE BACKGROUND

Step 2

The II Corinthians 12 passage is confusing even to some Bible scholars, let alone kids with little Bible background. Don't dwell too much on the part about being "caught up to the third heaven" other than to show that this was obviously something special God did for Paul. Yet God also allowed Paul to live with a "thorn" of some sort rather than give him a perfect and pain-free life. Try to show your group members that God isn't picking on us when things go wrong in our lives. Encourage them to look beyond the problems they have in order to see that God is still in control and will see them through whatever they are facing. Remind them that we live in an imperfect world, so we will experience occasional pain, disappointment, fear, and other negative emotions. Someday God will take care of all that and reward the people who remain faithful to Him. In the meantime, however, the only way we endure those things and continue to grow is by depending on His grace and power rather than our own strength.

Step 3

The challenge of Philippians 4:8 sounds simple enough. But people who barely know their way around a Bible may need help keeping their minds on true, noble, right, pure, lovely, admirable, excellent, and praiseworthy things. Try to have available some simple resources to hand out to your kids—a Bible-reading schedule for one of the Gospels, a list of your own favorite Scripture passages, a daily devotional book that looks like it might not bore them to death, or whatever. Explain that keeping one's mind on God by reading His Word is one of the best ways we can learn to maintain positive thoughts.

FELLOWSHIP & WORSHIP

Step 1

Have kids form small groups. Instruct the members of each group to share with each other their answers to the following questions:
• **What is your greatest strength?**
• **What is your greatest weakness?**
• **What can you do to serve God with your strength?**
• **What can you do to serve God with your weakness?**
• **What can God teach you through your strength?**
• **What can God teach you through your weakness?**

Step 4

Challenge your kids to think back over the past several sessions and all they've learned about habits, addictions, feelings, and moods. On a large piece of paper, write the following verse: "O give thanks to the Lord, for he is good; for his steadfast love endures forever" (Psalm 106:1). Provide creative materials for your kids. Instruct them to create a collage giving thanks to God for their strengths, weaknesses, various emotions, and the help He offers us to live a life that glorifies His name. Afterward, have the group sing a couple of praise songs, thanking God for His wisdom, love, and power. Close the session in prayer.

Step 3

Ask for volunteers to create and perform roleplays that depict the four basic types of moods described on Repro Resource 10. As volunteers perform each roleplay, the rest of the group will try to guess which mood is being depicted.

After volunteers have roleplayed all four moods, ask the following questions:
• **Which mood was easiest to recognize? Why?**
• **Which was the most difficult to recognize? Why?**
• **Which mood do you see most often in other students at school? Why do you think that is?**
• **If the mood that you see most often is a negative one, what do you think you could do to change that?**

Step 4

Say: **Ultimately, it's God who turns our difficulties or weaknesses into strengths or things that will glorify Him. However, there are some steps that we can take to turn our negative moods into positive ones.** Refer group members back to Repro Resource 11 and Philippians 4:8. Challenge them to apply the verse to the areas listed on Repro Resource 11 and to identify specific steps that they can take to change some of their negative mood factors to positive ones. Afterward, challenge your girls to take steps this week to put some of their ideas into practice. Close the session in prayer, asking God to give your girls the strength and willpower they need to take the steps they identified.

Step 2

Before getting into the Bible study, ask: **Can you think of a time when you endured pain temporarily and eventually became stronger for it?** Many guys are likely to have established exercise regimens in which they initially had extremely sore muscles and aching joints, yet kept working until their bodies shaped up and became much stronger. Others might have been injured in ball games, but tolerated the pain and went on to do well. Most guys are somewhat accustomed to dealing with physical pain. Use these illustrations as you move into spiritual areas. The same principles apply. No one enjoys being jabbed by a thorn as he is trying to accomplish something. But if there's no way to remove the thorn, the best remaining option is to persevere and go on in spite of the pain.

Step 3

Of all of the various mood factors listed on Repro Resource 11, perhaps most guys are lacking in the area of "Fuelers"—people who can encourage and help them. Guys tend to ignore the accumulated wisdom of their parents and discount much of what their teachers say "that won't be on the test." See how many of your group members can list five positive (Christian) male influences who genuinely care about them and will devote time and energy to seeing them succeed. For guys who come up short, try to have your own list of people to recommend they get in touch with. Your guys' teachers are concerned about their grades and their coaches are concerned about their athletic perfor-mance. See what you can do to hook your guys up with people who genuinely care about their personal and physical growth.

Step 3

Your group members are probably familiar with "musical chairs," but give them the opportunity to play "musical squares." Divide your room into four approximately equal sections; designate the sections with the quadrant labels from the Mood Management grid on Repro Resource 10. Play some music and have kids walk around, circling through all four grid segments. When the music stops, kids should stop in the grid where they're standing. Each time they stop, read one of the categories from Repro Resource 11. The kids in each grid segment should tell you how that category could possibly make them feel High Positive, Low Positive, High Negative, or Low Negative (depending on their location). Then start and stop the music again and move on to another factor. Some of these assignments will be more difficult than others, but kids should come up with answers for most of them.

Step 4

During the 1960's, freedom marches were quite popular, and music was a big part of them. By now, your group members should be seeing that freedom from their bad habits and addictions is possible, whether or not they have mastered them yet. So conclude this session (and this series) by singing. Have group members find songs that have specific references to being free. Don't worry about being on key. The main thing is to challenge kids to sing as if they really mean what they're saying.

Step 1

This session (and this series) may be more difficult than many of the things your group members have dealt with in the past. And usually, difficulty initiates complaints. Most kids don't want to do anything that's hard. So show them what some of their alternatives are. From the self-help section of a large video store, select two or three titles that are based on Eastern religions or New Age philosophies. Zip through them before the session and cue them up to particularly unusual suggestions for how to better oneself. Show these options to your group members and explain that the world will always offer "easy ways" to get better. Sometimes, in comparison, God's way to emotional and spiritual health may seem difficult. But the fact that God's way always works while the other alternatives are "empty words" (Ephesians 5:6) should inspire us to do what is hard when we need to. God always provides us the power to get through whatever we are facing (I Corinthians 10:13; Hebrews 4:15, 16).

Step 4

A group called "Acts of Renewal" does live shows along the themes you've discussed in this series. In lieu of booking them for a live performance, you might want to use some of the group's resources to conclude your series (or as a follow-up later to remind group members to keep thinking about these important issues). For additional information about what the group has to offer, contact Acts of Renewal, c/o St. John the Divine, 2450 River Oaks Boulevard, Houston, TX 77019, (713) 622-3600.

Step 1

Instead of having kids form small groups based on common interests, try a shorter opener. Pass around a couple of roses that have thorns on them. Give group members an opportunity to (carefully) examine the flowers. Then ask: **Do you think these roses would be prettier if they didn't have thorns? Why or why not?** Lead in to a discussion of the "thorn" that Paul talks about in II Corinthians 12.

Step 2

You can pare down the Bible study considerably by focusing solely on II Corinthians 12:7-10. Ask: **How might a "thorn in [the] flesh" keep someone from becoming conceited?** (When a person realizes that he or she is not powerful or self-sufficient enough to overcome a particular weakness or handicap, it may cause the person to rely on God's strength.) **Do you believe that you have a "thorn" in your life? If so, what do the Lord's words in II Corinthians 12:9 mean to you? Why?** Encourage several group members to respond.

Step 1

The opening exercise has little to do with the topic of the session, so you might want to replace it with a more competitive activity. Have kids form teams. Give the members of each team three minutes to list as many superheroes as they can think of. If some of your group members are into comic books, you may be surprised at how many different superheroes they come up with. When time is up, have each team read its list. Award prizes to the team that listed the most superheroes. Afterward, spend some time talking as a group about the "power sources" of various superheroes. For example, Spiderman got his powers when he was bitten by a radioactive spider. Superman came from another planet, which explains his extraordinary abilities. See how many other superhero "power sources" your kids can name. Use this activity to introduce the idea of turning weakness into strength.

Step 2

After you read II Corinthians 12:1-10, have kids form two teams for a "thorn in the flesh" relay. Assign each person a "thorn"—something that will hinder him or her during the race. For instance, one person might not be allowed to use her right foot at all during the race. Another person might be required to have both of his hands touching the ground at all times while he runs. Be creative with the "thorns" you assign. After the race, discuss as a group how Paul's "thorn" may have affected him.

Step 2
To help your younger kids better understand II Corinthians 12:1-10, supplement your discussion with the following questions:
• **Why would Paul have reason to boast about his own accomplishments?**
• **Why do you think God gave Paul grace to deal with his thorn, but didn't remove it?**
• **What would be the result of Paul's boasting about his weakness?**
• **What weakness do you have that God could turn into a strength for Him? How could He do that?**

Step 4
Have kids form teams. Give each team a piece of poster board and markers. Instruct each team to divide its poster board in half. On one side, team members should write or draw things that people in our society typically think about or fill their minds with; they should also write or draw possible results of thinking about such things. On the other side of the poster, team members should write out Philippians 4:8 and then draw what they think the world would be like if people filled their minds with these good things. After a few minutes, have each team display and explain its poster.

Step 2
Compare Jesus' words (quoted by Paul) in II Corinthians 12:9—"My power is made perfect in weakness"—with what Jesus said in His Sermon on the Mount—"Be perfect . . . as your heavenly Father is perfect" (Matthew 5:48). Ask: **Does God really expect perfection from us?** (Obviously, no human being is perfect. But perfection should be our goal. Too often we settle for far less than we're capable of doing. As we grow closer to God, we should raise our standards.) **What are some goals we can set for being more "perfect" in regard to our emotions, feelings, and moods?** Obviously, we shouldn't deny or repress negative emotions; yet we shouldn't be under the control of those emotions either. Let kids try to establish reasonable goals somewhere in between. Ask volunteers to share personal areas in which they've settled for less than perfection and have, in a sense, plateaued. Challenge kids to keep setting higher (but reasonable) goals for themselves, working toward the ultimate goal of perfection.

Step 4
Since one of the goals of this series has been an increased vulnerability toward one another, give kids a final opportunity to "bare their souls." Ask volunteers to share from one or more of the following categories: "Something I've learned during this series that's going to make a big difference in my life"; "One way I've changed during the past few weeks"; "A goal I've set for myself to accomplish in the near future"; "A bad habit or addiction I'm going to be working on." Challenge kids to be open. Also remind them of the commitment they agreed to in Session 1 (support, confidentiality, and so forth). End the session (and the series) with bold, positive testimonies of God's work in the lives of your kids.

Date Used:

Approx.
Time

Step 1: Common Interests _____
o Small Group
o Large Group
o Fellowship & Worship
o Media
o Short Meeting Time
o Urban
Things needed:

Step 2: A Thorny Issue _____
o Extra Action
o Heard It All Before
o Little Bible Background
o Mostly Guys
o Short Meeting Time
o Urban
o Combined Junior High/High School
o Extra Challenge
Things needed:

Step 3: Mood Management _____
o Extra Action
o Little Bible Background
o Mostly Girls
o Mostly Guys
o Extra Fun
Things needed:

Step 4: The HALT Method _____
o Small Group
o Large Group
o Heard It All Before
o Fellowship & Worship
o Mostly Girls
o Extra Fun
o Media
o Combined Junior High/High School
o Extra Challenge
Things needed:

Custom Curriculum Critique

Please take a moment to fill out this evaluation form, rip it out, fold it, tape it, and send it back to us. This will help us continue to customize products for you. Thanks!

1. Overall, please give this *Custom Curriculum* course (*Can't Help It?*) a grade in terms of how well it worked for you. (A=excellent; B=above average; C=average; D=below average; F=failure) Circle one.

   A   B   C   D   F

2. Now assign a grade to each part of this curriculum that you used.

a. Upfront article	A	B	C	D	F	Didn't use
b. Publicity/Clip art	A	B	C	D	F	Didn't use
c. Repro Resource Sheets	A	B	C	D	F	Didn't use
d. Session 1	A	B	C	D	F	Didn't use
e. Session 2	A	B	C	D	F	Didn't use
f. Session 3	A	B	C	D	F	Didn't use
g. Session 4	A	B	C	D	F	Didn't use
h. Session 5	A	B	C	D	F	Didn't use

3. How helpful were the options?
   - ❑ Very helpful
   - ❑ Somewhat helpful
   - ❑ Not too helpful
   - ❑ Not at all helpful

4. Rate the amount of options:
   - ❑ Too many
   - ❑ About the right amount
   - ❑ Too few

5. Tell us how often you used each type of option (4=Always; 3=Sometimes; 2=Seldom; 1=Never)

	4	3	2	1
Extra Action	❑	❑	❑	❑
Combined Jr. High/High School	❑	❑	❑	❑
Urban	❑	❑	❑	❑
Small Group	❑	❑	❑	❑
Large Group	❑	❑	❑	❑
Extra Fun	❑	❑	❑	❑
Heard It All Before	❑	❑	❑	❑
Little Bible Background	❑	❑	❑	❑
Short Meeting Time	❑	❑	❑	❑
Fellowship and Worship	❑	❑	❑	❑
Mostly Guys	❑	❑	❑	❑
Mostly Girls	❑	❑	❑	❑
Media	❑	❑	❑	❑
Extra Challenge (High School only)	❑	❑	❑	❑
Sixth Grade (Jr. High only)	❑	❑	❑	❑

6. What did you like best about this course?

7. What suggestions do you have for improving *Custom Curriculum*?

8. Other topics you'd like to see covered in this series:

9. Are you?
    ❑ Full time paid youthworker
    ❑ Part time paid youthworker
    ❑ Volunteer youthworker

10. When did you use *Custom Curriculum*?
    ❑ Sunday School   ❑ Small Group
    ❑ Youth Group   ❑ Retreat
    ❑ Other _____

11. What grades did you use it with? _____

12. How many kids used the curriculum in an average week? _____

13. What's the approximate attendance of your entire Sunday school program (Nursery through Adult)? _____

14. If you would like information on other *Custom Curriculum* courses, or other youth products from David C. Cook, please fill out the following:

    Name: _____
    Church Name: _____
    Address: _____
    _____

    Phone: (____) _____

    Thank you!